Taxcafe.co.uk Tax Guides

Landlord Interest

How to Protect Yourself from the
Big Cut in Tax Relief

By Carl Bayley BSc ACA
and
Nick Braun PhD

Important Legal Notices:

Taxcafe®
Tax Guide - "Landlord Interest"

Published by:
Taxcafe UK Limited
67 Milton Road
Kirkcaldy KY1 1TL
Tel: (0044) 01592 560081
Email: team@taxcafe.co.uk

Third edition, June 2017

ISBN 978-1-911020-15-8

Trademarks
Taxcafe® is a registered trademark of Taxcafe UK Limited. All other trademarks, names and logos in this tax guide may be trademarks of their respective owners.

Disclaimer
Before reading or relying on the content of this tax guide please read the disclaimer carefully.

Pay Less Tax!

...with help from Taxcafe's unique tax guides

All products available online at

www.taxcafe.co.uk

Popular Taxcafe titles include:

- *How to Save Property Tax*
- *Using a Property Company to Save Tax*
- *How to Save Inheritance Tax*
- *Landlord Interest*
- *Salary versus Dividends*
- *Using a Company to Save Tax*
- *Small Business Tax Saving Tactics*
- *Keeping it Simple: Small Business Bookkeeping, Tax & VAT*
- *Tax Planning for Non-Residents & Non Doms*
- *Tax Saving Tactics for Salary Earners*
- *Pension Magic*
- *Isle of Man Tax Saving Guide*
- *Tax-Free Capital Gains*
- *How to Save Tax*

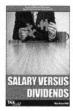

Disclaimer

1. This guide is intended as **general guidance** only and does NOT constitute accountancy, tax, investment or other professional advice.

2. The authors and Taxcafe UK Limited make no representations or warranties with respect to the accuracy or completeness of this publication and cannot accept any responsibility or liability for any loss or risk, personal or otherwise, which may arise, directly or indirectly, from reliance on information contained in this publication.

3. Please note that tax legislation, the law and practices of Government and regulatory authorities (e.g. HM Revenue & Customs) are constantly changing. We therefore recommend that for accountancy, tax, investment or other professional advice, you consult a suitably qualified accountant, tax advisor, financial adviser, or other professional adviser.

4. Please also note that your personal circumstances may vary from the general examples provided in this guide and your professional adviser will be able to provide specific advice based on your personal circumstances.

5. This guide covers UK taxation only and any references to 'tax' or 'taxation', unless the contrary is expressly stated, refer to UK taxation only. Please note that references to the 'UK' do not include the Channel Islands or the Isle of Man. Foreign tax implications are beyond the scope of this guide.

6. All persons described in the examples in this guide are entirely fictional. Any similarities to actual persons, living or dead, or to fictional characters created by any other author, are entirely coincidental.

7. The views expressed in this publication are the authors' own personal views and do not necessarily reflect the views of any organisation which they may represent.

About the Authors & Taxcafe

Carl Bayley is the author of a series of Taxcafe guides designed specifically for the layman. Carl's particular speciality is his ability to take the weird, complex and inexplicable world of taxation and set it out in the kind of clear, straightforward language that taxpayers themselves can understand. As he often says himself, "my job is to translate 'tax' into English".

In addition to being a recognised author, Carl has often spoken on taxation on radio and television, including the BBC's *It's Your Money* programme and the Jeremy Vine Show on Radio 2.

A chartered accountant by training, Carl is currently Chairman of the Tax Faculty of the Institute of Chartered Accountants in England and Wales and is also a member of the Institute's governing Council.

Nick Braun founded Taxcafe.co.uk in 1999, along with his partner, Aileen Smith. As the driving force behind the company, their aim is to provide affordable plain-English tax information to private individuals, investors, business owners and professional advisors.

Since then Taxcafe has become one of the best-known tax publishers in the UK and has won several business awards.

Nick has been involved in the tax publishing world since 1989 as a writer, editor and publisher. He holds a doctorate in economics from the University of Glasgow, where he was awarded the prestigious William Glen Scholarship and later became a Research Fellow. Prior to that, he graduated with distinction from the University of South Africa, the country's oldest university, earning the highest results in economics in the university's history.

Contents

Introduction

A couple of years ago the previous Chancellor of the Exchequer, George Osborne, dropped a huge tax bombshell on landlords.

Starting in April 2017, tax relief on interest and other finance costs paid by residential landlords is being phased out over a period of four years. In its place landlords will receive a "20% tax reduction".

Eventually residential landlords will not receive 40% or 45% tax relief on any of their interest payments and, as a result, many will see the amount of Income Tax they pay each year rise by thousands of pounds.

The way the change has been designed also means that many landlords who are currently basic-rate taxpayers will end up paying tax at 40% and some landlords will face other tax stings including losing their child benefit and Income Tax personal allowance and paying tax at the 45% additional rate on some of their income.

In this guide we explain how the tax relief restriction operates and what you can do to protect yourself from a much bigger tax bill.

In Chapters 1 and 2 we provide a brief overview of the changes and explain why we think the Government is hammering landlords.

In Chapters 3 and 4 we look at which types of property investor and which types of finance costs are affected by the change and the timetable for its introduction.

In Chapter 5 we explain the complexities of the new 20% tax reduction and the circumstances in which it is restricted.

Chapters 6 and 7 contain case studies showing how different landlords are likely to be affected by the reduction in their tax relief – during the current 2017/18 tax year and ultimately in 2020/21 when the tax relief cut will be in full force. As you will see, some landlords will come away relatively unscathed, others will suffer a catastrophic drop in income.

Chapter 8 contains some extra information for Scottish landlords, now that their Income Tax rates are set by the Scottish Parliament.

In Chapter 9 we examine how the reduction in tax relief, coupled with a future increase in interest rates, could wipe out some landlords' rental profits.

In Chapters 10 to 26 we turn to tax planning and explain how landlords can beat the tax increase by:

- Increasing the rent they charge
- Postponing tax deductible expenses
- Increasing tax deductible expenses (without suffering real economic loss)
- Accelerating finance costs
- Making pension contributions
- Reducing buy-to-let mortgages
- Selling properties
- Taking bigger dividends now (company owners)
- Emigrating
- Investing in other types of property
- Converting properties to a different use
- Using alternative investment structures
- Transferring properties to their spouses/partners
- Using a company (over 30 pages on this key issue)

Finally, in the last chapter we take a look at the new 'cash basis' for property businesses which could make it simpler for landlords to manage their tax affairs, although it also contains *another* potential sting in the tail for those with interest and other finance costs.

It's important to know about the cash basis because you will be forced to use it unless you actively opt out!

Scope of this Guide & Limitations

It is possible that further changes will be announced that affect some of the information contained in this guide.

Although the guide covers a fair amount of ground, it does not cover every possible scenario – that would be impossible without making it much longer and possibly much more difficult to digest.

Landlords come in many different shapes and sizes, so it is possible that some of the information contained in this guide will not be appropriate to your individual circumstances.

The main focus of this tax guide is *Income Tax* planning, i.e. how the reduction in tax relief for finance costs will affect the Income Tax paid by residential landlords and what they can do about it. Steps that you take to reduce one type of tax can have an adverse impact on your liability to pay other taxes.

There are also *non-tax* factors that have to be considered when taking action to reduce your tax bill. In some instances other considerations will outweigh any potential tax savings.

For all of these reasons it is vital that you obtain professional advice before taking any action based on information contained in this guide. The authors and Taxcafe UK Ltd cannot accept any responsibility for any loss which may arise as a consequence of any action taken, or any decision to refrain from taking action, as a result of reading this guide.

Scottish Taxpayers

The Scottish Parliament now has the power to set its own Income Tax rates and thresholds, although it cannot set the personal allowance or alter the tax rates applying to savings income or dividends.

Many of the examples in this guide illustrate how much tax landlords will pay in the years ahead, based on what the UK Government has already told us. The Scottish tax rates and thresholds are likely to vary and in Chapter 8 we explain the key differences.

3

The vast majority of the information contained in this guide is relevant to Scottish taxpayers. However, unless stated to the contrary, all examples, tables, calculations and illustrations are based on the assumption that the taxpayer concerned is not a Scottish taxpayer.

Landlords who are not Scottish taxpayers, but who invest in property in Scotland, will be unaffected by Scottish Income Tax rates. They will, however, pay Land and Buildings Transaction Tax on purchases of property in Scotland (instead of Stamp Duty Land Tax).

Accruals versus Cash

As we will see in Chapter 27, the new 'cash basis' has become the 'default' method for landlords to calculate their tax liabilities from 2017/18 onwards. However, despite this, we believe that most landlords will generally prefer to continue using the traditional accounting method under generally accepted accounting principles ('GAAP'), also sometimes known as the 'accruals basis', and will therefore opt out of the 'cash basis'.

We will look at the advantages and disadvantages of the 'cash basis' in Chapter 27 and, in particular, its impact on the restrictions in tax relief for interest and finance costs.

Throughout the rest of this guide, however, we will assume that landlords continue to use the traditional 'accruals basis'. Hence, unless stated to the contrary, all examples, tables, calculations and illustrations are based on the assumption that the taxpayer concerned is accounting for their rental income under GAAP.

Spouses and Partners

Please note that any references to a 'spouse' throughout this guide mean a legally married spouse or a registered civil partner. Unmarried partners are generally subject to a different tax treatment for most purposes.

Chapter 1

The Tax Change in a Nutshell

The Past

In previous tax years landlords could generally claim ALL their mortgage interest as a tax deductible business expense.

So if you had £20,000 of rental income, £10,000 of mortgage interest and, to keep things simple, no other expenses, your taxable rental profit would have been £10,000.

As a higher-rate taxpayer you would have paid 40% tax (£4,000) and as a basic-rate taxpayer you would have paid 20% tax (£2,000).

The Present and Future

Starting with the current 2017/18 tax year, the mortgage interest tax deduction is being phased out over a period of four years (see Chapter 4 for the timetable).

In its place landlords receive a basic-rate "tax reduction". Essentially what this means is an amount equal to 20% of your interest costs will be deducted from your final tax bill. Higher-rate taxpayers have always enjoyed 40% tax relief on their finance costs, so their tax relief is being halved.

For example, if when the interest deduction is fully phased out you have £20,000 of rental income and £10,000 of mortgage interest you will have a taxable rental profit of **£20,000**, not £10,000.

If you are a higher-rate taxpayer you will pay 40% tax on this profit (£8,000) and if you're a basic-rate taxpayer you'll pay 20% tax (£4,000). You'll then be given a "tax reduction" equal to 20% of your interest costs which in this case is £2,000 (£10,000 x 20%).

So if you're a basic-rate taxpayer you'll still pay £2,000 tax overall and will be unaffected by the change. If you're a higher-rate taxpayer you'll pay £6,000 tax overall – an increase of £2,000.

In a Nutshell

If you're a basic-rate taxpayer you will not have to pay more tax.

If you're a higher-rate taxpayer you can make a rough and ready estimate of how much extra tax you'll pay in 2020/21 and future tax years by multiplying your total finance costs by 20%.

This is because instead of getting 40% tax relief on your finance costs you will only get 20% in the future – a 20% cut in tax relief.

Thus, if your total finance costs are £10,000, your tax bill will eventually increase by £2,000 (£10,000 x 20%).

But it's Not Always that Simple

Because you will only be able to deduct a smaller and smaller amount of your interest costs from your rental income, your total taxable income could increase significantly over the next four tax years.

This means you could end up in a higher tax bracket than you have been in the past.

Thus some landlords who have always been basic-rate taxpayers could end up as higher-rate taxpayers following the change. As a result they could end up paying 40% tax instead of 20%.

In addition some landlords could see their income go over other key tax thresholds (e.g. £100,000 where the personal allowance is withdrawn or £150,000 where the additional rate of tax is payable).

In Chapter 6 we'll take a look at some case studies showing how different landlords are likely to be affected by the time the tax change has been rolled out fully in 2020/21.

What about the Current 2017/18 Tax Year?

If you're a higher-rate taxpayer this year you can make a very rough estimate of how much extra tax you'll pay because of the tax change by multiplying your total finance costs by 5%.

You are a higher-rate taxpayer this year if your taxable income is more than £45,000 (£43,000 in Scotland).

If you are still a basic-rate taxpayer this year, despite the fact that one quarter of your interest costs are no longer tax deductible, you will have no extra tax to pay.

Once again it's important to stress that these rough and ready estimates cannot be relied on by all taxpayers. If you end up in a higher tax bracket because some of your interest is no longer tax deductible, you could face a higher tax bill.

In Chapter 7 we'll take a look at some case studies showing how different landlords are likely to be affected this year.

Chapter 2

Why Is the Government Targeting Landlords?

Former Chancellor George Osborne (the man you should blame for this outrageous extra tax charge) staked his reputation on eliminating the UK's Budget deficit. His successor, Philip Hammond, is also a "fiscal conservative", which means he too doesn't like borrowing money.

Nevertheless, despite years of "austerity", the Government is still spending around £50 billion more per year than it takes in taxes.

On the tax raising front, the Conservatives tied their own hands by making the following pledge in their 2015 election manifesto:

"A Conservative Government will not increase the rates of VAT, Income Tax or National Insurance in the next Parliament."

As a result, they had to become more creative and tackle the deficit by introducing tax increases via the back door by "tackling tax avoidance and tax planning, evasion and compliance, and imbalances in the tax system".

Allowing landlords to claim tax relief on their mortgage interest was, apparently, one of those "imbalances". The 2015 Summer Budget document stated that:

"The current tax system supports landlords over and above ordinary homeowners. Landlords can deduct costs they incur when calculating the tax they pay on their rental income. A large portion of those costs are interest payments on the mortgage. Mortgage Interest Relief was withdrawn from homeowners 15 years ago. However, landlords still receive the relief. The ability to deduct these costs puts investing in a rental property at an advantage."

By likening landlords to homeowners it is clear that those in charge did not understand that landlords are proper business owners. It is, after all, a fundamental principle of taxation in most of the developed world that businesses can deduct all of their expenses when calculating their taxable profits.

There are some exceptions, for example entertainment spending is generally disallowed because the taxman believes meals at fancy restaurants and the like are more for personal pleasure than for genuine business purposes. Businesses also generally cannot claim immediate tax relief when they spend money on assets like cars and buildings: although UK tax law currently provides a generous annual investment allowance which allows full tax relief for many types of capital spending.

However, interest on loans used to buy business assets that produce taxable income (like rental properties) has always been considered a bread and butter "revenue expense", entitled to full tax relief.

It's Not Fair!

Do landlords run genuine businesses? The question isn't worth answering, as anyone who spends time managing a portfolio of rental properties will agree.

Nevertheless, the Government thought the change was fair because it would supposedly target "wealthier landlords" only:

"Tax relief for finance costs is particularly beneficial for wealthier landlords with larger incomes, as every £1 of finance cost they incur allows them to pay 40p or 45p less tax."

The Government aimed to rectify this by giving every landlord tax relief on their finance costs at the basic-rate only (i.e. 20%).

But surely if the Government wanted to target wealthy landlords only, it would have imposed higher taxes on those who don't have any mortgages at all? After all, if you own a lot of rental properties but also have a lot of mortgage debt you aren't necessarily wealthy but aspire to being wealthy.

Landlords are probably viewed as an easy target because most are currently enjoying healthy rental profits thanks to the historically low level of interest rates. The fact that many have also enjoyed healthy capital gains in recent years (even if only on paper) also means they can't expect much sympathy from their fellow taxpayers.

The fact that landlords are seen as an easy target was further confirmed by the announcement of a 3% increase in the rates of Stamp Duty Land Tax applying to purchases of additional residential property and the failure to extend the recent 8% cut in Capital Gains Tax to those disposing of residential property.

Apart from the desire to raise tax as sneakily as possible and level the playing field between homeowners and landlords, another reason for the tax change was to protect the banks from going bust again. Attempting to justify the change in the July 2015 Budget the Government stated that:

"The Bank of England has also noted in its recent Financial Stability Report that the rapid growth of buy to let mortgages could pose a risk to the UK's financial stability."

This seems to be a case of shutting the stable door after the horse has bolted. The time to clamp down on mortgage lending was before the 2008 financial crisis, i.e. when the banks were handing out cash hand over fist and offering products like 125% mortgages and self-certified loans.

Putting landlords under more financial pressure now will surely only increase the likelihood of mortgage defaults.

Although the restriction on landlord interest is deeply unfair, we don't expect any kind of u-turn. The legislation has been passed into law and is already in force for the current 2017/18 tax year.

Chapter 3

Who is Affected?

Residential Property Letting Businesses

The tax relief restriction affects *residential* property businesses only – commercial property businesses are unaffected by the change, as are furnished holiday letting businesses.

Of course, this is little consolation to the vast majority of small landlords who mostly invest in houses and flats. Investing in commercial property is a whole different ball game, requiring a different skill set.

Nevertheless, many business owners do own their own trading premises (e.g. an office, shop or factory unit) and will be relieved to hear that they can continue to claim full tax relief on all of their mortgage interest.

It is also important to note that the tax relief restriction does not just apply to interest on buy-to-let mortgages – it also applies to almost all of the finance costs incurred by a residential property letting business.

More specifically, the legislation restricts the tax relief on "dwelling-related loans". Generally speaking, dwelling-related loans are loans used to generate income from dwelling houses.

So if you take out a loan to buy a car for use in your residential property letting business, the tax relief on your interest payments will be restricted.

Similarly, if you take out a loan to buy an office to run your residential property letting business, the tax relief on your interest payments will be restricted. The fact that the office may be a commercial property is irrelevant – the loan will be treated as a dwelling-related loan because it is for the purpose of generating income from dwelling houses.

The restriction also applies to loan arrangement fees and other finance costs.

Under general accounting principles, the costs of obtaining long-term finance (e.g. loan arrangement fees) should be spread over the life of the loan.

This will lead to some practical difficulties as many costs incurred *before* the change started to take effect on 6th April 2017 should be claimed in later accounting periods. We will look at this issue in more detail in Chapter 14.

Property Developers

The interest restriction does not apply to businesses that develop property for sale or deal in property – it applies only to residential property letting businesses, i.e. businesses that generate income from renting out residential property.

In other words, if you borrow money to buy a property with the intention of doing it up and selling it on for a profit, the tax relief on your finance costs will not be restricted.

What is a Dwelling House?

There is no definition of "dwelling house" in the legislation, so the phrase takes its ordinary meaning. According to HM Revenue and Customs the distinctive characteristic of a dwelling house is its ability to provide the facilities required for day-to-day private domestic existence.

Most landlords who rent out flats and houses earn income from dwelling houses and will therefore have their tax relief restricted.

Nursing homes and hotels which are run as a trade and offer other services are not generally considered to be dwelling houses.

Running a guest house is also usually considered to be a trade. Hence, whilst interest relief on a loan to buy, or finance, a guest house must be restricted to the proportion of the property used for business purposes, it will not generally be necessary to apply the further restrictions discussed in this guide.

Student accommodation is more of a grey area. Halls of residence owned by universities are generally considered not to be dwelling houses. However, houses in multiple occupation (HMOs) that provide bedrooms and communal kitchens and living rooms are generally considered to be dwelling houses.

Remortgaging

What happens if you borrow against a rental property that you already own? As has always been the case, what matters is how you *use* the money, not how the loan is secured.

For example, let's say you already own a residential property and borrow against it to buy a commercial rental property. You will continue to be entitled to full tax relief on your interest payments, i.e. you are not affected by the tax change.

But if you use the loan to invest in another residential rental property you are, as you would expect, subject to the new tax relief restriction.

And if you use the money for personal reasons, for example to pay your child's school fees, there will generally be no tax relief on the interest payments, as has always been the case. There is one important exception here, however. Tax relief is available when you borrow against a rental property *up to its original value when first rented out*, no matter what the borrowed funds are used for. Even if the borrowed money is used for personal reasons the interest still qualifies for tax relief.

For example, let's say you inherit a flat worth £200,000 and begin renting it out. If you then borrow against the property (up to £200,000), all the interest payments will qualify for tax relief, even if you use the money for personal reasons, for example to pay school fees.

However, for the current 2017/18 tax year and future tax years the amount of tax relief is restricted, as it is for any other residential property loan.

Mixed Properties

What happens if you own a mixed property with both a commercial and residential component, for example a shop which has a flat on top?

If there is a single loan over the entire property the finance costs have to be apportioned. The interest relating to the shop remains fully tax deductible; interest on the flat is restricted.

Mixed Property Businesses

Complexity may arise where a landlord owns a mixture of commercial and residential properties. Where each property has its own mortgage the calculations are relatively straightforward: interest relating to commercial properties remains fully tax deductible; interest on residential properties is restricted.

However, an apportionment is required when a single loan facility is used to buy both residential and commercial properties, or where borrowings are used to buy assets for use in the combined business, e.g. cars, equipment and business premises.

Companies Unaffected

The new rules for landlords do not apply to companies, so if your residential properties are held inside a company there is generally no restriction to the tax relief the company can claim on its interest payments.

It doesn't matter whether the company carries on the property business directly or in partnership. However, the exemption does not apply where the company carries on the business in a fiduciary or representative capacity (i.e. as a nominee rather than the beneficial owner).

The new rules do, however, apply to partnerships and limited liability partnerships, as well as certain trusts.

Corporate Interest Relief Generally

In the March 2016 Budget a change was announced to limit the Corporation Tax relief companies receive for interest and other finance costs from 1st April 2017. Most small company owners will be unaffected because all groups will be able to deduct up to £2 million per year of net interest expenses in the UK. Above this threshold, the new rules generally cap interest deductions to 30% of taxable earnings before interest, taxes, depreciation and amortisation (EBITDA) in the UK.

We will take a closer look at the pros and cons of using a company to invest in residential property in Chapter 23.

More Information on Interest and Finance Costs

For more information on which interest and finance costs are eligible for tax relief if you are a landlord, see the Taxcafe.co.uk guide *'How to Save Property Tax'*.

It is important to understand that the tax changes being rolled out over the next few years do not alter **which** interest and finance costs may be claimed by a landlord: they only alter the **rate** of tax relief available.

Chapter 4

The Timetable

The good news is the withdrawal of tax relief on mortgage interest is being rolled out gradually.

This year (the 2017/18 tax year that started on 6th April 2017) 75% of your mortgage interest is fully tax deductible and you are entitled to a 20% "basic-rate tax reduction" for the remainder.

The timetable is as follows:

- 2017/18   75% deducted as normal, 25% as basic-rate reduction
- 2018/19   50% deducted as normal, 50% as basic-rate reduction
- 2019/20   25% deducted as normal, 75% as basic-rate reduction
- 2020/21   All finance costs relieved at basic-rate only

From 2020/21 onwards you will not be able to claim any of your interest as a tax deductible expense, just the 20% tax reduction.

Example
Oz has a salary just in excess of the higher-rate tax threshold each year. He also receives rental profits of £40,000 before deduction of interest costs which amount to £20,000 each year. Oz will pay tax as follows on his rental income:

	2016/17	**2017/18**	**2018/19**	**2019/20**	**2020/21**
Profit before interest	40,000	40,000	40,000	40,000	40,000
Less: Interest	20,000	15,000	10,000	5,000	0
	(100%)	(75%)	(50%)	(25%)	Nil
Taxable profit	20,000	25,000	30,000	35,000	40,000
Tax @ 40% (A)	8,000	10,000	12,000	14,000	16,000
Basic rate relief on	0	5,000	10,000	15,000	20,000
Equals: (B)	0	1,000	2,000	3,000	4,000
Tax payable (A-B)	£8,000	£9,000	£10,000	£11,000	£12,000

As we can see, by the time we get to 2020/21 the tax Oz pays on his rental income will have increased by £4,000.

In Chapter 1 we mentioned that some landlords who are higher-rate taxpayers can make a rough and ready estimate of how much extra tax they'll pay in 2020/21 by simply multiplying their interest costs by 20%.

This holds true in Oz's case – his total interest costs are £20,000 and multiplying by 20% we get £4,000.

The Current 2017/18 Tax Year

We also said that many higher-rate taxpayers can make a rough and ready estimate of how much extra tax they'll pay this year (2017/18) because of this change by simply multiplying their interest costs by 5%.

Once again this holds true in Oz's case – his total interest costs are £20,000 and multiplying by 5% we get £1,000 which is the amount of extra tax he pays this year.

These rough and ready estimates cannot be relied on by all taxpayers. If you end up in a higher tax bracket because some of your interest is no longer tax deductible, you could face a higher tax bill.

In Chapter 7 we'll take a look at some case studies showing how different landlords are likely to be affected this year.

Preparing for the Change

Some landlords remain blissfully unaware of the withdrawal of tax relief on their mortgage interest. Others have been preparing for the change since it was announced in 2015, with some taking fairly drastic action, including transferring existing properties into a limited company.

However, it's important to point out that you should not panic and do something that you will later regret.

Fortunately, this year only one quarter of your interest costs will be denied full tax relief and the tax sting will only actually be felt in January 2019 when tax payments for the current 2017/18 tax year fall due.

Nevertheless, because the changes are so profound and because property is essentially a long-term investment, it is necessary to find out the likely impact on your property business and decide what, if anything, you intend to do.

For example, some landlords may decide to start building a cash reserve to help cover future tax bills. Others may decide to hold off buying new properties until they fully understand how the interest restriction will affect them or hold off re-mortgaging existing properties to release equity.

Those who feel the interest change will have a serious impact on their property businesses may decide to sell properties and may then need to start preparing as soon as possible. For example, some landlords may need to let certain mortgage deals run their course before selling to avoid early repayment fees.

Where a property is to be sold unoccupied it may also be necessary to wait until existing lease agreements have run their course before selling. It may also be desirable to spread property sales over several years to save Capital Gains Tax.

We don't think many landlords will take the "nuclear option" and sell up completely. Most will simply take the tax hit on the chin. At present many landlords are enjoying healthy rental profits thanks to low interest rates and may still be better off than they were a few years ago, despite the tax change. In some parts of the country landlords have also enjoyed excellent capital growth and may decide that a higher Income Tax bill is worth paying in return for less heavily taxed capital gains.

However, this could all change if interest rates eventually start to rise or property values level off or decline. At that point some landlords may feel that their investments are no longer viable.

Too Late to Beat the Stamp Duty Surcharge

Some of the planning strategies covered later in this guide involve property transfers which may be subject to Stamp Duty Land Tax or Land and Buildings Transaction Tax (in Scotland).

In the first edition of this guide we mentioned that readers considering these strategies needed to implement their plans before 1st April 2016 in order to avoid the 3% surcharge for purchases of additional residential property.

However, it is now too late to beat the 3% surcharge, where it applies, and it may have to be weighed against the potential tax savings you hope to achieve.

Property in Wales

Note also that a new tax, Land Transaction Tax, will apply instead of Stamp Duty Land Tax to purchases or transfers of property in Wales after 31st March 2018. The rates for the new tax are to be announced by 1st October 2017. Sadly, if the experience in Scotland is anything to go by, the Welsh Government will probably also introduce a 3% surcharge similar to the rest of the UK; but time will tell whether this gloomy forecast proves correct!

Chapter 5

The 20% Tax Reduction: How it Works

Although interest expenses are no longer a fully tax deductible expense you can still claim a 20% "tax reduction". So if during the current 2017/18 tax year you have £10,000 of mortgage interest 25% of it is no longer a tax deductible expense (£2,500) but your final Income Tax bill will be reduced by £500 (£2,500 x 20%).

In 2020/21 none of your interest will be deductible but your final Income Tax bill will be reduced by £2,000 (£10,000 x 20%).

The tax reduction is not always calculated as 20% of your finance costs. There are some restrictions to prevent landlords receiving too much relief. The tax reduction is calculated as 20% of the *lowest* of:

- The finance costs not allowed as a deduction

- The profits of the property business, after deducting any brought forward property losses

- Your "adjusted total income" (total income less savings income, dividends and your personal allowance)

Looking at the first bullet point, this number is 25% of your finance costs in 2017/18, 50% in 2018/19, 75% in 2019/20 and 100% thereafter.

The second bullet point could apply if you have unusually low rental profits in any particular year, e.g. if you have unusually large repair costs. It may also apply if there are significant losses brought forward from previous tax years.

The third bullet point may apply if you have a relatively low level of income overall.

If bullet points two or three apply and restrict the tax reduction, the excess finance costs will be carried forward to future tax years.

Example

In 2020/21 Latif has salary income of £40,000 and rental income of £20,000. He also has other property expenses of £3,000, so his taxable rental profit is £17,000. He also pays £7,000 in mortgage interest but none of this is deducted when calculating his taxable rental profit.

His tax reduction is calculated as 20% of the lowest of:

- *His finance costs = £7,000*

- *His taxable rental profits = £17,000*

- *Adjusted total income (£40,000+£17,000-£12,500) = £44,500*

(We assume the personal allowance in 2020/21 is £12,500)

In this example Latif can claim a tax reduction equal to 20% of his finance costs and is unaffected by the other restrictions.

Example revised

The facts are the same as before except Latif has unexpectedly high expenses (e.g. repair costs) of £15,000, so his taxable rental profit is £5,000. His tax reduction is calculated as 20% of the lowest of:

- *His finance costs = £7,000*

- *His taxable rental profits = £5,000*

- *Adjusted total income (£40,000+£5,000-£12,500) = £32,500*

In this example Latif can claim a tax reduction equal to 20% of his taxable rental profits: £5,000 x 20% = £1,000.

The excess finance costs (£2,000) will be carried forward to the next tax year and added to his finance costs for that year.

So if he also has £7,000 of finance costs in the next tax year his tax reduction will be 20% of £9,000 (unless his rental profits or adjusted total income are lower).

Example revised again

The facts are the same as in the first example except Latif doesn't have any salary income, just rental income. His tax reduction is calculated as 20% of the lowest of:

- *His finance costs = £7,000*

- *His taxable rental profits = £17,000*

- *His adjusted total income (£17,000 - £12,500) = £4,500*

Latif can claim a tax reduction equal to 20% of his adjusted total income: £4,500 x 20% = £900. The excess finance costs (£2,500) can be carried forward to the next tax year.

Landlords with Losses

The 20% tax reduction may also be restricted if you have rental losses brought forward from previous tax years:

Example

During the current 2017/18 tax year Ivana has a salary of £50,000 and gross rental income of £20,000. She pays £7,000 in mortgage interest and 75% of this (£5,250) is allowed as a tax deduction. She also has other property expenses of £3,000, so her taxable rental profit for the year is £11,750. She has rental losses of £19,000 brought forward from previous tax years, so her taxable rental profit is reduced to zero. The remaining loss of £7,250 is carried forward to next year.

Her tax reduction is calculated as 20% of the lowest of:

- *Her disallowed finance costs (£7,000-£5,250) = £1,750*

- *Her taxable rental profits = £0*

- *Adjusted total income (£50,000 + £0 - £11,500) = £38,500*

(£11,500 is the personal allowance for the current 2017/18 tax year)

Ivana cannot claim any tax reduction this year but the £1,750 of unrelieved finance costs can be carried forward to the next tax year.

Example continued

In 2018/19 Ivana once again has a salary of £50,000 and rental income of £20,000. She pays £7,000 in mortgage interest and 50% of this (£3,500) is allowed as a tax deduction. She has other property expenses of £2,500, so her taxable rental profit for the year is £14,000. She also has rental losses of £7,250 brought forward from the previous tax year, so her taxable rental profit is reduced to £6,750.

Her tax reduction is calculated as 20% of the lowest of:

- *Finance costs not allowed (£3,500 + £1,750) = £5,250*

- *Her taxable rental profits = £6,750*

- *Adjusted total income (£50,000+£6,750-£11,750) = £45,000*

Ivana will receive a tax reduction of 20% of all of her unrelieved finance costs (£3,500 from this year and £1,750 from last year). Her tax bill will be reduced by £1,050 (£5,250 x 20%).

(The personal allowance for 2018/19 has been estimated at £11,750)

Summary

For the vast majority of landlords calculating the 20% tax reduction will not create any problems – they will simply multiply their disallowed finance costs by 20%.

However, the tax reduction may be smaller if you have smaller than normal rental profits (for example if your repair costs for the year are high) or if you have rental losses from previous years.

The tax reduction may also be smaller if you have very low adjusted total income (e.g. if you have very little income from other sources and small rental profits).

If your tax reduction is restricted, the excess finance costs will be carried forward to future tax years.

Chapter 6

How Much Tax Will You Pay?
Case Studies

In this chapter and the next, with the help of some case studies, we'll look at how the mortgage interest tax change will affect different property investors.

In the next chapter we'll look at how much extra tax you're likely to pay this year (2017/18) compared with last year (2016/17).

For this chapter though, we will jump straight to the 2020/21 tax year when the restriction will have full force. We don't know what tax rates will look like in 2020/21 but the Government has promised to increase the higher-rate threshold to at least £50,000 by this date and to increase the personal allowance to at least £12,500. So we'll use these numbers.

Of course, there could be other tax changes along the way that may affect the outcomes. In particular, Scottish taxpayers are likely to be subject to different tax rates (see further in Chapter 8).

Case Study 1 – No Impact

Pearl is a retired widow who receives a pension of £20,000 per year and net rental income (before deducting her finance costs) of £18,000. She pays £6,000 interest on her buy-to-let mortgages, so her "true" rental profit is £12,000.

Assuming there was no restriction to her mortgage interest tax relief, her total taxable income would be £32,000. The first £12,500 would be tax free and the rest would be taxed at 20% producing a tax bill of £3,900.

But with none of her interest allowed as a tax deductible expense her taxable income will be £38,000, resulting in a tax bill of £5,100. However, she will also be entitled to a tax reduction equal to 20% of her mortgage interest (£1,200), so her final tax bill will still be £3,900.

Comment – Pearl is completely unaffected by the tax change because her total taxable income remains below the £50,000 higher-rate threshold, i.e. none of her income ends up being taxed at 40%.

Those who will find themselves in a similar position include taxpayers who have relatively small amounts of income from other sources and small property portfolios, e.g. many retirees and non-working spouses.

Case Study 2
From 20% Tax to 40% Tax

Dave is a full-time landlord with rental income of £75,000. He pays £25,000 interest on his buy-to-let mortgages and has other property related expenses of £10,000, resulting in a true rental profit of £40,000.

Assuming no restriction to his mortgage interest relief, his total taxable income would be £40,000. The first £12,500 would be tax free and the rest would be taxed at 20%, producing a tax bill of £5,500.

But with none of his interest allowed as a tax deduction his taxable income will be £65,000. £15,000 will now be subject to higher-rate tax at 40%. He'll also be entitled to a tax reduction equal to 20% of his interest. His final tax bill will be £8,500.

Comment – Dave's tax bill is £3,000 higher thanks to the change. Because he cannot deduct his mortgage interest his taxable income increases by £25,000 and he becomes a higher-rate taxpayer. As a result he pays an additional 20% tax on £15,000 of his rental income.

This case study reveals the fact that some landlords who are currently basic-rate taxpayers will become higher-rate taxpayers when they can no longer deduct their mortgage interest.

You can perform a rough-and-ready "back of the envelope" calculation to see if you will be affected in a similar way. First find out how much you currently pay in mortgage interest (usually found in box 26 of the UK property part of your tax return). Then add this back onto your taxable income (salary, dividends, rental profits etc). If the total exceeds the higher-rate threshold (expected to be around £50,000 by 2020/21) you are likely to end up with a higher tax bill.

Case Study 3
An Extra Tax Sting – Loss of Child Benefit

If Dave is also a parent and his family receives child benefit he could face an extra tax sting: the High Income Child Benefit Charge.

This kicks in when the highest earner in the household has income over £50,000. Once your income reaches £60,000 all of the family's child benefit is effectively lost thanks to the tax charge.

The £50,000 threshold does not increase each year with inflation so there's a good chance it will still be £50,000 in 2020/21.

Because his mortgage interest will no longer be a tax deductible expense Dave's taxable income will increase from £40,000 to £65,000, so he will go from paying no child benefit tax charge to having all the family's child benefit effectively taken away.

How much extra tax will Dave pay? We don't know what child benefit rates or rules will apply in the years ahead but, based on current rates, Dave could end up paying anywhere from £1,076 (one child), to £3,214 (four children), or even more (£712 extra for each further qualifying child), in additional tax, on top of the £3,000 extra tax he pays by becoming a higher-rate taxpayer.

Comment – *Many landlords will find themselves in a similar position, i.e. with taxable income below £50,000 under the current rules but over £50,000 when their interest is no longer tax deductible. In some cases having to pay the High Income Child Benefit Charge will more than double the amount of extra tax you have to pay.*

Case Study 4
Higher-Rate Taxpayer – Best Case Scenario

Maureen is a landlord who also works full time. In 2020/21 she earns a salary of £60,000 and net rental income of £40,000 (before deducting her finance costs). She pays £12,000 interest on her buy-to-let mortgages so her true rental profit is £28,000.

First let's calculate how much tax she would pay if there was no restriction to her mortgage interest tax relief. Because her salary already takes her over the £50,000 higher-rate threshold, she would pay 40% tax on her entire rental profit – £11,200.

However, with none of her interest allowed as a tax deductible expense she will have an additional £12,000 taxed at 40%, increasing her tax bill by £4,800. She will also be entitled to a tax reduction equal to 20% of her mortgage interest (£2,400), so her total tax bill will increase by £2,400.

Comment – *This is the best case scenario for a higher-rate taxpayer: her tax bill increases by an amount equivalent to 20% of her finance costs (because she's getting 20% tax relief instead of 40% tax relief). However, she doesn't get pushed into a higher tax bracket.*

Case Study 5
Personal Allowance Taken Away

Colleen is a landlord who also works full time. In 2020/21 she earns a salary of £60,000 and net rental income of £65,000 (before deducting her finance costs). She pays £25,000 interest on her buy-to-let mortgages so her true rental profit is £40,000.

First we calculate how much tax she would pay if there was no restriction to her mortgage interest tax relief. With taxable income of £100,000 she would pay £27,500 in tax. The first £12,500 would be tax free; the next £37,500 would be taxed at 20% and the final £50,000 at 40%. (This includes the tax on her salary collected under PAYE.)

However, with none of her interest allowed as a tax deductible expense she will have taxable income of £125,000 and her personal allowance will be completely withdrawn.

(Your personal allowance is gradually withdrawn when your income exceeds £100,000. For every additional £2 you earn you lose £1 of allowance. So if the personal allowance is £12,500 in 2020/21 someone with income of £125,000 or more will lose their whole personal allowance.)

Tax on income of £125,000 comes to £42,500. However, Colleen will also be entitled to a tax reduction equal to 20% of her mortgage interest (£5,000), so her final tax bill will be £37,500 – an increase of £10,000!

***Comment** – Colleen suffers a double tax whammy: She no longer gets 40% tax relief on her mortgage interest and loses her personal allowance. Each tax sting costs her an additional £5,000.*

Quite a few landlords could find themselves in a similar position in 2020/21, in particular those with large but quite heavily geared property portfolios, i.e. those whose taxable rental profits will increase sharply when their interest payments are no longer tax deductible.

Case Study 6
Existential Event – Income Drops by 50%

It's the 2020/21 tax year and Katerina is a full-time landlord who owns a portfolio of rental properties producing net rental income of £125,000 per year. This is after deducting all the expenses of the business except her mortgage interest.

Her portfolio is heavily geared and her interest payments are £75,000 per year. Thus her true rental profit is £50,000 per year.

We'll assume Katerina has no other taxable income but does receive around £2,500 in child benefit and is the highest earner in her household.

Assuming there was no restriction to her mortgage tax relief, Katerina would have taxable income of £50,000 in 2020/21 (if she had any more income she would be a higher-rate taxpayer). The first £12,500 would be tax free thanks to her personal allowance and the final £37,500 would be taxed at just 20% producing a total Income Tax bill of £7,500.

Furthermore, because her taxable income would not exceed £50,000 she would not have to pay the child benefit tax charge and would keep all of her £2,500 child benefit.

Her total after-tax disposable income would therefore be £45,000.

Now let's see how Katerina will fare under the restriction to mortgage interest tax relief. Because her mortgage interest will no longer be a tax deductible expense she will have a taxable rental profit of £125,000.

With this much income she will lose all of her Income Tax personal allowance. Thus the first £37,500 will be taxed at 20% and the remaining £87,500 at 40% resulting in tax of £42,500.

Against this she will be able to claim a tax reduction of 20% of her mortgage interest (£15,000) leaving her with a total tax bill of £27,500.

She will also have to pay the full child benefit charge and will effectively lose £2,500 of income, so her final after-tax disposable income will fall from £45,000 to £22,500:

£125,000 net rent - £75,000 interest - £27,500 tax = £22,500

Comment – *With her after-tax income falling by 50% it is unlikely that Katerina will be able to cover her household expenses and she will probably have to take drastic action to shore up her finances.*

This example illustrates that the main victims of the tax change will not be "wealthier landlords with larger incomes", as the Government would have us believe. Instead it will be landlords who have big buy-to-let portfolios but significant amounts of debt, i.e. those who earn significant amounts of rental income but have fairly modest rental profits.

These landlords will end up being forced to pay tax at 40% (and possibly 45%) on profits that do not exist and may face other tax penalties such as the loss of their Income Tax personal allowance and child benefit.

Case Study 7
Landlord with Dividend Income

Sinead is a landlord who also owns a graphic design company. In 2020/21 she takes a tax-free salary of £12,500 out of her company and dividends of £40,000.

She also earns a rental profit of £35,500 before deducting her interest costs. She pays £12,000 interest on her buy-to-let mortgages, so her true rental profit is £23,500.

However, with her mortgage interest no longer tax deductible, her taxable rental profit will be £35,500. Along with her salary of £12,500 this will take her income up to £48,000.

Because this is still below the £50,000 higher-rate threshold all of her taxable rental profit will still be taxed at 20%, with an offsetting tax reduction of 20% on her mortgage interest. So at first glance it looks like she is unaffected by the tax change.

Where Sinead will feel the sting, however, is on her dividend income. Dividends are always treated as the top slice of income.

The first £2,000 of her dividend income will be tax free thanks to the dividend allowance, but this will take her income up to the £50,000 higher-rate threshold. (The dividend allowance is expected to fall from £5,000 to £2,000 in April 2018.)

All of her remaining dividend income will be taxed at the 32.5% higher rate.

The end result is that because her taxable rental profits increase by £12,000, this will push £12,000 of her dividend income over the higher-rate threshold where it will be taxed at 32.5% instead of 7.5% – an increase of 25%.

Thus her final tax bill will increase by £3,000 (£12,000 x 25%).

Comment – *Many company owners will find themselves in a similar position. The July 2015 Budget contained two major tax bombshells for company owners who are also landlords. First dividend tax rates were increased significantly. Second it was announced that tax relief on mortgage interest would be restricted.*

Many landlords who are higher-rate taxpayers will see their tax bills increase by an amount equivalent to 20% of their mortgage interest. However, for many company owners with dividend income the tax hit is 25%. For example, a company owner with £20,000 of buy-to-let interest could end up paying £5,000 more tax in 2020/21.

Case Study 8
Company Owner Denied Tax Reduction

In 2020/21 Louise receives dividends of £50,000 from her family's pub company, although she does not work there. She also owns a flat from which she receives net rental income of £12,000 (before deducting her finance costs). She pays £7,000 interest, so her true rental profit is £5,000.

With none of her mortgage interest allowed as a tax deduction her taxable rental profit will increase by £7,000 to £12,000. All of her rental profit will still be tax free as it will be covered by her £12,500 personal allowance. However, an additional £7,000 of her dividend income (that would have been covered by her personal allowance) will be taxed at 32.5% instead of 0% – a tax increase of £2,275.

And what about her 20% tax reduction? Remember from Chapter 5 this is calculated as 20% of the *lowest* of:

- Finance costs not allowed = £7,000

- Taxable rental profits = £12,000

- Adjusted total income (£12,000 - £12,500) = £0

Her dividends are not included in her adjusted total income so when we subtract her personal allowance from her taxable rental profit her adjusted total income is reduced to zero (it cannot be reduced below zero).

Thus Louise cannot claim any tax reduction!

Comment – *For someone who earns a modest rental profit of £5,000 a tax increase of £2,275 is significant.*

Taxpayers who could find themselves in a similar position include silent shareholders who do not receive any salary income and have relatively small amounts of income from property.

Case Study 9
Additional Rate Tax

In 2020/21, Ranjit, a full time landlord, receives net rental income of £200,000 after deducting all expenses except interest. His total allowable interest amounts to £75,000, giving him a true rental profit of £125,000.

Assuming no restriction to his mortgage interest, his total taxable income would be £125,000. The first £37,500 would be taxed at 20% and the rest at 40%, giving him a tax bill of £42,500.

However, with none of his interest allowed as a tax deduction, Ranjit's taxable income is increased to £200,000. The first £37,500 will be taxed at 20%, the next £112,500 at 40%, and the final £50,000 at the additional rate of 45%.

This gives Ranjit a total tax liability of £75,000, but he remains entitled to a tax reduction equal to 20% of his interest, i.e. £15,000. His final tax bill will therefore be £60,000.

Ranjit suffers an overall tax increase of £17,500. This represents an additional charge of 20% on the first £25,000 of his mortgage interest (taking him up to the additional rate tax threshold of £150,000) plus 25% on the remaining £50,000.

Comment – *Once the landlord's total taxable income exceeds the additional rate tax threshold of £150,000, the impact of the change in interest relief increases from 20% to 25%.*

This will affect many landlords with large residential property portfolios.

Chapter 7

How Much Will You Pay this Year (2017/18)?

In the previous chapter we examined the full impact of the tax change on a number of landlords in 2020/21. In this chapter we'll look at the tax payable by a variety of landlords this year (2017/18), when just one quarter of their finance costs will be disallowed, and compare it with the tax they paid last year (2016/17).

In Chapter 1 we pointed out that, if you're a higher-rate taxpayer, you can make a very rough estimate of how much extra tax you'll pay this year because of the tax change by multiplying your total finance costs by 5%.

So if your total finance costs are £20,000 your tax bill will be £1,000 higher than it would have been if your interest was fully deductible.

However, this doesn't mean you'll pay £1,000 more tax than you did last year. This year the personal allowance has been increased from £11,000 to £11,500 and the higher-rate threshold has been increased from £43,000 to £45,000 (unless you live in Scotland). These tax cuts will help offset any increase in your Income Tax bill caused by the cut in interest tax relief.

That's the good news. The bad news is the cut in interest relief could hit you harder than our rough estimate if your taxable income ends up being pushed over one of the following Income Tax thresholds:

- £50,000   Child benefit charge
- £100,000   Personal allowance withdrawal
- £150,000   Additional rate threshold

Note, in the case studies that follow we use the term "net rental income" which is your rental income minus all your tax deductible property expenses, except interest and other finance costs.

Case Study 1 – Income Tax Bill Falls

Ivanka doesn't work but earns net rental income of £30,000 from some flats. Her interest costs are £10,000 per year. Last year (2016/17) her total taxable income was £20,000 and her Income Tax bill was £1,800.

This year (2017/18) her Income Tax bill will be just £1,700 thanks to the more generous personal allowance. Although one quarter of her interest costs are disallowed, the 20% tax reduction completely makes up for her smaller interest deduction.

Case Study 2
Income Tax Bill Stays the Same

Melania earns a salary of £40,000 and has net rental income of £20,000 and pays £10,000 interest on her mortgages. Last year her taxable income was £50,000 and her Income Tax bill was £9,200.

This year one quarter of her interest (£2,500) is disallowed so her taxable income increases to £52,500. The Income Tax payable is £9,700 less a £500 tax reduction for disallowed interest – £9,200 in total. Melania's Income Tax bill is the same as last year.

She'll also pay a tiny bit less National Insurance although, if she has children, she may lose one quarter of her child benefit if she is the highest earner in the household.

Case Study 3
From 20% to 40% Tax ... but only a Small Tax Increase

Donald is a full-time landlord with net rental income of £65,000. He pays £25,000 interest on his mortgages. Last year his taxable rental profit was £40,000 and his Income Tax bill was £5,800.

This year one quarter of his interest (£6,250) is disallowed so his taxable rental profit increases to £46,250 and goes over the higher-rate threshold. The Income Tax payable is £7,200 less a £1,250 tax reduction for the disallowed interest – £5,950 in total.

Donald has become a higher-rate taxpayer but his tax bill is just £150 higher than last year.

Case Study 4
Personal Allowance Withdrawal

Jared has a salary of £75,000, net rental income of £45,000 and pays £15,000 interest on his mortgages. Last year his taxable income was £105,000 and his Income Tax bill was £32,200.

This year one quarter of his interest (£3,750) is disallowed so his taxable income increases to £108,750, resulting in further withdrawal of his personal allowance. The Income Tax payable is £33,950 less a £750 tax reduction for disallowed interest – £33,200.

Jared's Income Tax bill increases by £1,000. He also pays around £190 more National Insurance on his salary.

Case Study 5
Heavily Geared Portfolio

Let's see how Katerina from Chapter 6 fares this year (she's the landlord with large borrowings who will see her income cut in half by 2020/21). Her net rental income is £125,000 and her interest payments are £75,000. Last year her taxable rental profit was £50,000 and her Income Tax bill was £9,200.

This year 25% of her interest (£18,750) is disallowed so her taxable income increases to £68,750. The Income Tax payable is £16,200 less a £3,750 tax reduction for disallowed interest: £12,450 in total.

Thus Katerina's tax bill will increase by £3,250. She will also be subject to the maximum Child Benefit Charge in 2017/18 which will cost her an additional £2,500. The total extra tax is £5,750.

Case Study 6
Company Owner

Anton is a company owner and earns a salary and net rental income of £40,000. He pays £10,000 in buy-to-let mortgage interest and gets his company to pay him a dividend of £40,000. Last year he paid Income Tax of £13,175.

This year one quarter of his interest (£2,500) is disallowed so his taxable income increases from £70,000 to £72,500. The Income Tax payable is £13,700 less a £500 tax reduction for disallowed interest – £13,200 in total.

Anton's tax bill increases by just £25! Although some of his interest is no longer deductible, this is offset by this year's more generous tax thresholds.

Summary

What these case studies show is that every landlord is different. How much extra tax you will pay this year, if any, will vary according to how much non-property income you have, how big your borrowings are and whether your family receives child benefit.

The case studies also reveal that the tax sting this year (2017/18) will be relatively modest for many landlords.

Having said this, it's important to note that, to keep things simple, we assumed that all of the individuals earn the same income this year as last year. However, it's possible their salaries and rental income will be a bit higher this year just because of inflation, making them no better off in *real* terms.

If their incomes are higher than in the case studies, so too will be their Income Tax bills. So the examples all, arguably, understate the amount of tax the landlords will pay this year.

Chapter 8

Scottish Landlords

The Scottish Parliament now has full power over Income Tax rates and thresholds applying to most forms of income received by Scottish taxpayers, including rental income.

However, the Scottish Parliament has no power over:

- Income Tax rates on dividends and savings income
- Personal allowances (and their withdrawal where income exceeds £100,000)
- The High Income Child Benefit Charge
- National Insurance
- Corporation Tax
- Capital Gains Tax
- The 'tax base' – i.e. the way in which a person's total taxable income is calculated

In most cases, an individual will be a Scottish taxpayer if they are a UK resident whose main home is in Scotland.

Individuals who are not Scottish taxpayers will continue to pay UK Income Tax rates on all their taxable income: including any rental profits on Scottish properties.

Implications for Scottish Landlords

Scottish landlords will continue to be subject to the restrictions on interest relief discussed throughout this guide. Their taxable rental profits will be calculated in exactly the same way as anyone else: but the rate of tax payable on those profits may differ.

Scottish landlords will also continue to receive the same 20% tax reduction for their interest costs as everyone else. At present, it is not clear what will happen to this reduction if the basic rate of tax is changed for Scottish taxpayers.

Scottish taxpayers who use a company to invest in property pay the same rate of Corporation Tax in their company as everyone else and also pay the same rates of tax on any dividends they receive.

Scottish landlords continue to pay Capital Gains Tax on any property sales (or transfers) at exactly the same rates as all other UK resident taxpayers.

Scottish Income Tax 2017/18

In 2017/18 Scottish Income Tax is the same as the rest of the UK with one important exception: the higher-rate threshold is frozen at £43,000 (the threshold is £45,000 in the rest of the UK).

As a result, Scots will pay Income Tax as follows on most types of income in 2017/18:

- 0%   on the first   £11,500
- 20%   on the next   £31,500
- 40%   above   £43,000
- 45%   above   £150,000

Scots who earn over £45,000 will pay £400 more tax than those who live in the rest of the UK.

Example
Robert lives in Scotland, earns a salary of £60,000, has net rental income of £40,000 and pays £20,000 interest on his mortgages. Last year (2016/17) his taxable income was £80,000 and his Income Tax bill was £21,200.

This year one quarter of his interest (£5,000) is disallowed so his taxable income increases to £85,000. The Income Tax payable is £23,100 less a £1,000 tax reduction for disallowed interest – £22,100 in total.

Robert's Income Tax bill increases by £900. If he lived anywhere else in the UK (where the higher-rate threshold is £45,000 instead of £43,000) his Income Tax bill would have increased by just £500.

He will also pay around £190 more National Insurance.

Future Tax Years

The higher-rate tax threshold in Scotland will not be increased in line with the UK higher rate tax threshold.

This means the "tartan tax gap" is likely to increase over the next few years as the UK Government raises the higher-rate threshold to £50,000.

At best the Scottish higher-rate tax threshold will increase in line with inflation, as measured by the consumer prices index. If we estimate inflation at 2% over the next few years, this means the Scottish higher-rate threshold will be just £45,631 by 2020/21 (when it is expected to stand at £50,000 for other UK taxpayers). This will cost Scottish taxpayers with taxable income of £50,000 or more an extra £874 in Income Tax.

However, even increases in line with inflation are by no means guaranteed. The threshold was originally supposed to increase in 2017/18 but was instead frozen at £43,000.

Chapter 9

What Will Happen if Interest Rates Increase?

Thanks to historically low interest rates many landlords are currently enjoying healthy rental profits.

If these low interest rates persist many landlords will be able to absorb the higher Income Tax they have to pay now that the tax relief on their mortgage interest is being restricted.

But what if interest rates increase significantly? Most economic commentators don't think this will happen, at least not in the near future. Most believe that, if and when interest rates do go up, the increases will be small and very gradual.

It's impossible to predict when interest rates will increase and by how much. However, because property is a long-term investment it's probably a good idea to "stress test" your portfolio to see how you would cope with a big increase in interest rates, especially when the tax relief on your mortgage interest is restricted.

Example – Before the Tax Change
Campbell is a landlord and also earns a salary of £50,000. Before the mortgage interest tax change came into force, he bought a property for £100,000 with a £75,000 interest only mortgage costing 3% (i.e. £2,250 per year). He receives rental income of £6,000 per year and his other tax deductible expenses come to £1,000. His true rental profit is therefore £2,750 and as a higher-rate taxpayer he pays 40% tax (£1,100), leaving him with a total after-tax rental profit of £1,650.

Example – After the Tax Change
Let's now move forward to 2020/21 and assume the facts are exactly the same except Campbell cannot claim a tax deduction for his mortgage interest. His taxable rental profit will now be £5,000 resulting in a tax liability of £2,000. However, he'll also be entitled to a tax reduction of £450 (£2,250 x 20%), reducing his overall tax bill on this property to £1,550. His after-tax rental profit will therefore fall from £1,650 before the tax change to £1,200.

Obviously Campbell will be upset to be paying more tax but he is still making a positive rental return on the property. However, let's see what happens if interest rates have increased significantly by 2020/21.

Example continued

The facts are exactly the same except Campbell ends up paying 5% interest in 2020/21 (£3,750). His taxable rental profit will still be £5,000 resulting in a tax liability of £2,000. He'll also be entitled to a tax reduction of £750 (£3,750 x 20%), reducing his overall tax bill on the property to £1,250. However, his after-tax rental profit will now be £0:

Rental income	*£6,000*
Less:	
Interest	*£3,750*
Other costs	*£1,000*
Net tax	*£1,250*
After-tax profit	*£0*

Campbell is now receiving no return from the property on the income side and must rely purely on capital growth instead.

He may be prepared to accept this outcome if he thinks the property will continue to rise in value.

However, he won't have any rental income left over to build any sort of contingency fund to protect against any unexpected costs and to cover any periods when the property is empty.

He will have to rely on his other income to cover any unexpected property expenses – possibly acceptable for just one property but his finances could be placed in a precarious position if he owns many properties.

In this example we assumed that the interest rate on Campbell's mortgage increases from 3% to 5%. Although this would be a significant increase from current levels, interest rates have been far higher in the past. Just before the 2008 financial crisis mortgage rates of 6-7% were not uncommon.

We also assumed that Campbell's rental income does not increase between now and 2020/21. Rent increases may reduce much of the tax sting landlords will face, as we shall see in Chapter 11.

Summary

With mortgage interest rates at historically low levels many landlords will be able to absorb higher tax bills as the tax relief on their interest is gradually restricted.

However, if interest rates were to increase significantly at some point in the future, some landlords, in particular those with high loan to value ratios, may see all their rental profits disappear due to higher interest and tax charges.

Chapter 10

How to Beat the Tax Increase

In the chapters that follow we'll take a look at some of the things landlords can do to reduce the impact of the tax change including:

- Increasing rent
- Tax deductible spending on properties
- Accelerating finance costs
- Making pension contributions
- Paying off mortgages
- Selling properties
- Taking bigger dividends now (company owners)
- Emigrating
- Investing in other types of property
- Converting properties to a different use
- Using alternative investment structures
- Transferring properties to spouses
- Using a company

We suspect that many landlords will simply take the tax hit on the chin. Why? Because although they'll end up with less income than before, their properties will continue to produce positive rental profits thanks to the low level of interest rates.

Remember before interest rates were reduced following the 2008 financial crisis it wasn't uncommon for property investors to make rental *losses* year after year. They were happy to accept this outcome because their properties were rising in value and generating attractive capital gains.

Many property investors do not depend on their properties for income and invest primarily for capital growth. These landlords may be happy to accept a smaller after-tax rental income if their properties continue to rise in value.

Those that do depend on their properties for income may find that there is still no alternative investment that produces better returns.

However, this could all change if interest rates increase significantly at some point in the years ahead. If that happens more landlords may feel the need to sell up or take other action.

Those landlords who will feel the need to act soon are those who have large property portfolios and large amounts of debt. Remember Katerina from Case Study 6 in Chapter 6? She saw her after-tax income fall from £45,000 to £22,500. In Chapter 17 we'll take a look at whether she should sell some of her properties.

Chapter 11

Increasing Rent to Cover Tax Bills

In the days following the July 2015 Budget, press articles stated that many landlords were intending to increase the rent they charge to cover the tax increase. In other words, many landlords were intending to pass on the tax increase to their tenants.

In this chapter we'll show you how much extra rent you would have to charge to do this and whether this strategy is viable.

Example
Matt earns a salary of £60,000 and also receives rental income of £20,000. He pays £10,000 interest on his buy-to-let mortgages and we'll ignore his other property costs to keep the example simple.

In 2016/17, before the tax change, his interest was fully tax deductible so his taxable rental profit was £10,000. After paying 40% tax he was left with £6,000.

Now let's move forward to 2020/21 and assume Matt's rental income has increased to £23,333.

He'll pay 40% tax (£9,333) but will also be entitled to a tax reduction equal to 20% of his mortgage interest (£2,000). All in all Matt will be left with £6,000:

£23,333 rent - £10,000 interest - £7,333 net tax = £6,000

Matt is completely unaffected by the tax change because the increase in his rental income completely absorbs the increase in his tax bill.

By how much will your rental income have to increase to cover the extra tax you'll pay in 2020/21? As a rule of thumb, if you're a higher-rate taxpayer, you can calculate the extra rent you will need by multiplying your interest bill by one third.

Matt in the above example pays £10,000 interest so he must increase his rental income by £3,333 (£10,000/3) to cover the extra tax he will pay. He'll pay 40% tax on this extra rent which will leave him with an additional £2,000 – exactly the amount of tax relief he loses on his mortgage interest.

This is very much a "back of the envelope" calculation and will not apply to all taxpayers. For example, those who also end up paying the child benefit charge or losing their personal allowance will have to charge even more rent.

Note too that, although Matt ends up with the same amount of rental income after tax, we have not taken account of inflation. Matt may need to charge even more rent to cover the general increases in his other property costs and his own cost of living.

Will Landlords Be Able to Increase their Rents?

Matt will have had to increase the rent he charges by around 4% per year between 2016 and 2020 to keep his after-tax rental income exactly the same. The increases will have to be even greater than this to compensate for inflation as well.

As every landlord knows, the ability to increase rent varies from one part of the country to another. Some landlords will be able to increase the rents they charge, others will not.

Rents are already high in many parts of the UK and further increases may only be possible if wages increase. However, if wages increase significantly this may also put pressure on the Bank of England to raise interest rates, which in turn will squeeze landlords' profits.

So it's by no means certain that landlords will be able to maintain the status quo by simply increasing the rents they charge.

However, some landlords in some parts of the country will probably be able to claw back at least some of the extra tax they will pay by increasing rents.

Chapter 12

Postponing Tax Deductible Expenses

If you think you will end up in a higher tax bracket as the tax relief on your interest is reduced, it may be possible to save tax by postponing spending on your properties.

For the current 2017/18 tax year, the key tax thresholds are:

- £45,000*   Higher-rate threshold
- £50,000   Child benefit charge
- £100,000   Personal allowance withdrawal
- £150,000   Additional rate threshold

* £43,000 in Scotland

For example, if you expect to be a basic-rate taxpayer in 2017/18 (when 25% of your interest is no longer tax deductible) but a higher-rate taxpayer in 2018/19 (when 50% will no longer be deductible) it may be possible to save tax by postponing spending until 2018/19.

This way you may be able to enjoy 40% tax relief instead of 20% on the spending you postpone.

Example
Ron is a full-time landlord who earns net rental income of £75,000. This is after deducting all his property expenses except his interest costs which come to £40,000. He has no other income.

In 2017/18 three quarters of Ron's interest costs will be tax deductible so he will have a taxable rental profit of £45,000. The higher-rate threshold in 2017/18 is £45,000 so Ron will be a basic-rate taxpayer (i.e. he will pay no more than 20% tax on his profits).

In 2018/19 half of Ron's interest costs (£20,000) will not be tax deductible which means he'll have a taxable rental profit of £55,000. We don't know what the higher-rate threshold will be in 2018/19 but based on announcements to date we'll assume that it will be £46,500.

With a taxable rental profit of £55,000 Ron will be a higher-rate taxpayer and pay 40% tax on £8,500 of income (£55,000 - £46,500).

Now let's say Ron wishes to spend £5,000 replacing the kitchen in one of his properties. If he spends the money in 2017/18 he will enjoy 20% tax relief (£1,000) but if he spends the money in 2018/19 he will enjoy 40% tax relief (£2,000).

Ron saves £1,000 by postponing his spending.

Marginal Tax Rates

In our last example, Ron saved tax by postponing allowable expenditure to a year in which he had a higher top rate of tax (i.e. he went from being a basic rate taxpayer to a higher rate taxpayer). We refer to the effective tax rate applying to the top slice of a taxpayer's income as their 'marginal tax rate'.

The 'marginal tax rate' is the rate at which each £1 of additional income will be taxed, or the rate at which each £1 of additional expenditure will provide tax relief (where it is fully tax deductible). It is a key concept in tax planning and we will therefore refer to it many times throughout the rest of this guide.

The Other Key Tax Thresholds

The £50,000 Threshold

If you expect your taxable income to rise above £50,000 as the tax relief on your interest is further reduced, you may be able to save tax by postponing tax deductible spending on your properties.

If you're the highest earner in a household that receives child benefit you have to pay the High Income Child Benefit Charge once your income rises above £50,000. Once your income reaches £60,000 you face the maximum charge and all the family's child benefit is effectively withdrawn.

Based on current child benefit rates, if you end up in the £50,000-£60,000 tax bracket in 2018/19 you could suffer an effective marginal Income Tax rate of around 51% if you have one child (higher if you have more children).

So if you can postpone some of your 2017/18 spending until 2018/19, you may be able to reduce your taxable income and enjoy 51% or more tax relief!

The £100,000 Threshold

If you expect your taxable income to rise above £100,000 as the tax relief on your interest is further reduced you may also be able to save tax by postponing spending.

This is because taxpayers with income over £100,000 suffer from having their personal allowances withdrawn. The personal allowance is withdrawn at the rate of £1 for every £2 of income you have over £100,000.

We don't know yet what the personal allowance will be in 2018/19 but, based on announcements to date, we will assume that it will be £11,800. So once your taxable income rises above £123,600 you will have no personal allowance left.

If you end up in the £100,000-£123,600 tax bracket in 2018/19 you will suffer an effective marginal Income Tax rate of 60%. Thus if you can postpone some of your spending until then you may be able to reduce your taxable income and enjoy 60% tax relief!

The £150,000 Threshold

If you expect your taxable income to rise above £150,000 as the tax relief on your interest is further reduced, you will become an additional rate taxpayer and pay Income Tax at 45%.

You may be able to save tax by postponing tax deductible spending on your properties but the savings may be quite modest. You will enjoy tax relief at 45% instead of 40% which isn't a huge difference.

What Types of Spending Can be Postponed?

If you spend money on your properties, the expense is normally treated as either a repair or an improvement.

Repairs are immediately tax deductible and will save you Income Tax. Obvious examples of repairs are things that require urgent attention: broken windows, faulty boilers, etc. This type of repair is normally dealt with by the landlord immediately so discretionary tax planning doesn't come into the picture.

Improvements are not so good from a tax-saving perspective because tax relief is only provided when the property is sold and will only save you up to 28% Capital Gains Tax. Improvements are generally new features that were not present in the property before and therefore increase its value: extensions, attic conversions, etc.

Between these two extremes are repairs that provide full Income Tax relief AND may increase the value of your property and/or increase its rental potential.

Examples include: New kitchens, new bathrooms, double glazing, and most decorating costs. Many property investors think of these items as improvements but often they are in fact fully tax-deductible repairs... provided you follow the rules. To be treated as repairs, it is important that you replace old items with broadly equivalent new items and do not add something new that was not present before.

For example, replacing a tatty old kitchen is usually a tax-deductible repair. If you add extra kitchen units or sockets, these additional items will be improvements. Replacing a pea-green bathroom is a tax-deductible repair. Installing a shower or downstairs toilet where there wasn't one before is an improvement.

When replacing old items it is also important that you do not substantially upgrade the quality – that would be an improvement. However, it IS acceptable to install items that are of superior quality when they are simply the nearest modern equivalent, for example, replacing old single glazing with double glazing.

Although this is a tax-efficient way to spend your rental profits, there is no guarantee that this type of spending will always increase the value of your property or your rental income (or enough to make it worthwhile). There's also clearly a limit to the amount of this type of repair you can carry out, so it is not a permanent solution to your Income Tax problem.

See the Taxcafe.co.uk guide *'How to Save Property Tax'* for more details on which items qualify as tax deductible repairs.

Other Spending You May be Able to Postpone

To postpone expenditure, there needs to be a degree of discretion over the timing. This will not always be the case: a broken window will usually need to be replaced immediately.

Other expenditure is related to a specific time period and will generally have to be claimed as an expense of that period, regardless of when you actually pay it. Examples include ground rent, insurance premiums and utility bills (where these are paid by the landlord). (The position on items of this nature will differ under the 'cash basis', so we will return to this point in Chapter 27.)

Nonetheless, there are some items which allow for a degree of discretion over the timing of your expenditure.

Replacements

Under the new 'replacement furniture relief', all landlords can claim the cost of replacing movable items provided in fully or partly furnished residential properties: such as furniture, carpets, white goods and electrical equipment.

Such expenditure could often be postponed by a short period in order to obtain a better rate of tax relief. For example, you might be able to get a few extra months out of an old carpet: provided that there are no safety issues involved!

There might even be a case for extending the life of faulty equipment, even if the overall pre-tax cost will be greater.

Example

Hermione is a basic-rate taxpayer in 2017/18 but, due to the further reduction in her interest relief, she will be a higher-rate taxpayer in 2018/19. There is a faulty washing machine in one of her rental properties and it will inevitably need replacing in the near future. A replacement will cost £600 but a temporary repair costing £75 will keep the machine going into the 2018/19 tax year.

If Hermione replaces the machine in 2017/18, she will get tax relief at just 20%, giving her a net, after tax, cost of £480.

If she has the temporary repair carried out in 2017/18 and then replaces it in 2018/19, her total pre-tax expenditure will be more (£675), but her tax relief will amount to £15 in 2017/18 (£75 x 20%) and £240 in 2018/19 (£600 x 40%). Her total cost, after tax, is thus £420.

The saving in this example is not very much (just £60), but it does illustrate the fact that an overall saving can sometimes arise even when the total pre-tax cost is greater.

Car Sales and Equipment Purchases

Residential landlords are generally unable to claim capital allowances on furniture and equipment within their rental properties. They may, however, claim capital allowances on cars and other equipment purchased for their own use within their business.

Equipment, other than cars, which is purchased for business use, will generally attract immediate 100% tax relief under the annual investment allowance: although the relief claimed must be reduced to reflect any private use.

Cars used in the business generally only attract writing down allowances at either 8% or 18%, depending on the level of their CO_2 emissions, and these allowances must again be reduced to reflect private use of the vehicle.

When a car with business use is sold, however, there will generally be a balancing allowance (again reduced to reflect private use).

Hence, landlords facing an increase in their marginal tax rate can save tax by postponing the purchase of new equipment and/or the sale of a car used in their business.

Example

Due to the further reduction in his interest relief, Harry's taxable income will increase from £100,000 in 2017/18 to £120,000 in 2018/19, giving him a marginal tax rate of 60% (see above).

Harry wants to buy a new laptop for £1,000, which he will use 90% in his business. He also wants to replace his car, which is used 75% for business purposes.

Harry's car cost £35,000 in 2012 and is now worth just £10,000. By the end of 2016/17, he had claimed writing down allowances of £11,932 on the car (before the reduction to reflect private use), leaving £23,068 of unrelieved expenditure carried forward.

When Harry buys his new laptop, he will be able to claim £900 under the annual investment allowance (£1,000 x 90%).

When he sells his car, he will be able to claim a balancing allowance of £13,068 (£23,068 - £10,000), reduced to £9,801 to reflect private use.

Harry's total claim will thus amount to £10,701 (£900 + £9,801) and, if he does all this in 2017/18, he'll save £4,280 in Income Tax (at 40%).

But, if Harry waits until 2018/19 to buy his laptop and sell his car, his saving will be £6,420 (at 60%), i.e. £2,140 more!

Note that we have assumed Harry disclaims the writing down allowance on his old car in 2017/18, in order to maintain his balancing allowance at the same level on a sale in 2018/19. This will often be worth doing where a car is to be sold the following year and the taxpayer's marginal Income Tax rate is set to increase.

Harry has saved tax by postponing the sale of his old car to a year in which he has a higher marginal tax rate and this is what has produced most of his additional tax saving (£1,960 out of the total additional saving of £2,140).

He has also made a further small additional tax saving of £180 by postponing the purchase of his new laptop.

However, it will seldom be worth postponing the purchase of a new car, even when the landlord's marginal Income Tax rate is expected to increase. This is because buying the new car in the earlier year will produce writing down allowances in both years.

For example, if Harry buys a new model costing £40,000 with 75% business use and eligible for 8% writing down allowances, then buying it in 2017/18 will give rise to a writing down allowance of £2,400 in that year (£40,000 x 8% x 75%). The unrelieved expenditure of £36,800 (£40,000 less 8%) carried forward will then give rise to a writing down allowance of £2,208 in 2018/19 (£36,800 x 8% x 75%).

Harry's total tax saving over the two years will then be £2,285 (£2,400 x 40% = £960 in 2017/18, plus £2,208 x 60% = £1,325 in 2018/19).

This is £845 better than the saving of £1,440 (£2,400 x 60%) in 2018/19 if he had postponed his purchase of the car until then.

Naturally, where the old car is being traded in for the new car, the two transactions will have to take place at the same time and it will be necessary to assess whether there still remains an overall saving to be made by postponing them. Usually there will be: for example, in Harry's case, postponing the sale saves an extra £1,960, whereas postponing the purchase reduces his savings by £845. Overall though, postponing the trade in saves him a net sum of £1,115.

But the best of all worlds (where possible) would be for Harry to buy his new car in 2017/18 and sell his old car in 2018/19.

Remember, it is postponing the sale of the old car which produces the tax saving, not postponing the purchase of the new car!

Some Words of Warning

Most sales of cars which are used in a business will produce a balancing allowance. Beware, however, that balancing charges may arise instead in some instances (especially sales of cars with very low CO_2 emissions). Where a balancing charge is likely to arise, it will generally be preferable to accelerate the sale to an earlier tax year where the landlord still has a lower marginal Income Tax rate.

Note also that postponing the purchase of some cars to after 31st March 2018 will reduce the amount of capital allowances available on the new car. The cars affected are those with CO2 emissions between 50g/km and 75g/km or between 110g/km and 130g/km

For more details on replacement furniture relief and capital allowances claims for landlords, see the Taxcafe.co.uk guide *'How to Save Property Tax'*.

Self-Employed Business Owners

If you also own another unincorporated business, over and above your residential property business, you will have even more flexibility when it comes to postponing your tax deductible expenses in order to save tax.

For example, a self-employed tree surgeon (who is also a landlord) may be able to postpone buying a new van until next year (2018/19) if he or she thinks they will end up in a higher tax bracket next year thanks to the tax relief restriction. A self-employed web designer may be able to save tax by postponing new computer expenditure until next year... and so on.

Postponing tax deductible spending on either your property business or your other unincorporated business will achieve exactly the same result which is to reduce your taxable income in 2018/19.

No Change in Tax Bracket

Finally, it's important to always remember that you will only save tax by postponing tax deductible expenses IF you end up in a higher tax bracket in 2018/19 compared with 2017/18 – only some taxpayers will find themselves in this situation.

For example, if you have taxable income of £40,000 this year and £55,000 next year you will be able to save tax by postponing expenses (because you will go from being a basic-rate taxpayer to a higher-rate taxpayer). But if you have taxable income of, say,

£60,000 this year and £75,000 next year you will not save any tax by postponing expenses (because you'll be in the same tax bracket in both years).

A further complication is that most taxpayers simply do not know what their marginal tax rate is this year or next year. However, if your income is relatively stable (as it is for many who earn salaries and rental income) it should be fairly easy to estimate.

Chapter 13

Increasing Tax Deductible Expenses

A very easy way to save tax is simply to increase your business expenditure. But this, in itself, would be pointless, because ....

Bayley's Law

The truly wise investor does not seek merely to minimise the amount of tax payable, but rather to maximise the amount of wealth remaining after all taxes have been accounted for.

In other words, the sensible objective is generally to increase your profit after tax rather than simply reducing your tax bill. Going out and spending extra money on your business just to save tax is usually nonsense. This is why most of our advice regarding expenditure is about the timing of the expenditure, or the type of expenditure, and not about spending extra money just for the sake of it.

But there are a few exceptions where additional expenditure may be justified.

In Chapter 12 we looked at some of the discretionary expenditure on your properties which may enhance the value of the property, or its rental yield, and yet still be allowed as deductible repairs expenditure.

Here are a few other ideas:

Payments to Family

If you have a partner, spouse, or child with little or no taxable income of their own, then it may be possible to pay them for any services which they provide to your property business.

For example, you might pay a spouse for repairs and maintenance work or pay one of your children for assisting you with managing your portfolio.

There are a few words of caution which we must sound here, however.

Firstly, the family member must genuinely be providing an appropriate level of services to your business to justify the payments being made. Otherwise, any deduction which you claim may be denied or restricted.

Secondly, unless the family member is providing the services as part of a business which they already run, you are likely to have to treat them as an employee. If they are your first employee (most landlords do not have any other employees) this is likely to create a great deal of extra admin work for you: including the need to operate the notoriously burdensome 'RTI' (real time information) procedures for payroll purposes. You may also need to set up an 'auto-enrolment' pension scheme in some cases.

Thirdly, the payments which you make will represent taxable income in the payee's hands. However, if the payee has no other taxable income, it will generally be possible to pay them up to £8,164 without creating any tax liabilities for them; sometimes up to £11,500 (at 2017/18 rates).

Fourthly, payments in excess of £8,164 made to a family member who has to be treated as an employee might lead to employer's National Insurance liabilities for you, although these can now be avoided in many cases.

Fifthly, in the case of children, you can generally only employ them if they are at least 13 years old (sometimes 14, depending on local by-laws) and, for all children under school leaving age, there are also legal limits on the amount of work which they can do: which, in turn, limits the amount which you can justify paying them.

Sixthly, payments made to a family member with their own existing business will need to include VAT if the payee is already registered for VAT, or if the payments themselves push their gross annual income over the VAT registration threshold (currently £85,000). This will create an additional 20% VAT cost which the landlord will not be able to recover and would frequently mean that the payments have a detrimental effect overall.

Lastly, the payments must actually be made. Mere notional 'book entries' will not usually suffice. Spouses, partners and children aged 16 or more might subsequently make payments to you for 'room and board', and children might start paying for their own clothes, outings, meals out, etc, but these things are an entirely separate matter.

Nonetheless, despite all of these potential drawbacks, making payments to your family for services provided to your business could still save you a great deal of tax, especially where your own marginal tax rate is set to rise as a consequence of the reduction in interest relief.

Example
Belinda has a residential property portfolio which produces annual profits before interest of £120,000. Her interest costs total £80,000, giving her a true rental profit of £40,000 and making her a basic rate taxpayer in the previous 2016/17 tax year.

She has two very young children plus an older child, Suzy, who was born in March 2002, but who will remain in full-time education throughout the period covered by this example. Belinda is therefore able to claim child benefit of around £2,500 in 2017/18.

Belinda's husband, Dama, has his own small business as an 'odd job man' which produces an annual profit of around £20,000. He also carries out most of the repairs and maintenance work on Belinda's properties but, up to now, he has never charged her for this.

As a consequence of the reduction in interest relief, Belinda's taxable income and effective marginal tax rate are expected to increase as follows:

Year	Taxable Income	Tax Rate
2017/18:	*£60,000*	*(65%)*
2018/19:	*£80,000*	*(40%)*
2019/20:	*£100,000*	*(40%)*
2020/21:	*£120,000*	*(60%)*

See Chapter 12 for explanations of how these marginal tax rates arise.

In the past there was no point in Belinda paying Dama for the work he did on her properties. She would have obtained tax relief at 20% and he would have had a combined Income Tax and National Insurance liability at 29%: an overall tax cost of 9%.

From 2017/18 onwards, however, Belinda starts paying Dama £10,000 per year for the work he does on her properties. This increases Dama's total tax and National Insurance liability by £2,900 each year but will lead to greater savings for Belinda.

At the same time, Belinda also starts to employ Suzy part-time to help her in the business at an annual salary of £5,000.

Belinda now has additional deductible expenditure of £15,000 each year: but it's all in the family!

In 2017/18, this will enable Belinda to keep all her child benefit and also save tax at 40%: a total saving of £8,500.

In 2018/19 and 2019/20, Belinda will save tax at 40%: or £6,000 each year.

In 2020/21, Belinda will save tax at an effective rate of 60%: i.e. £9,000.

In total, over a four year period, Belinda will save £29,500. After offsetting the additional tax and National Insurance paid by Dama, the overall net saving for the family amounts to £17,900.

Unlike some of the 'one-off' items discussed in Chapter 12, payments to a spouse or partner may provide a means to continue saving tax consistently year on year. If Belinda and Dama continue as they are after 2020/21, the payments she makes to him will continue to save them £3,100 every year.

Payments to children are generally a less permanent solution. Eventually, Suzy will probably have some taxable income of her own and the saving will diminish. Even so, if Suzy remains a basic rate taxpayer, the payments would often still continue to provide an overall net saving of 20% or 40%, depending on the level of Belinda's taxable profits. Plus there's always those younger siblings to consider in the future!

For a great deal more information on making tax deductible payments to spouses, partners and children, see the Taxcafe.co.uk guide 'Small Business Tax Saving Tactics'.

Property Management Fees

Some landlords have entered into arrangements whereby they pay property management fees to some sort of connected entity, such as their own company, a family partnership, or a spouse or partner.

Generally, we feel that these arrangements are highly risky, as they lack any commercial substance. Where, however, the connected entity has a genuine property management business with other, unconnected, clients, then the arrangement may be valid. Having unconnected employees (i.e. non-family members) within the property management business would also give it more validity.

In Chapter 26, we will look at the potential benefits of using your own property management company for this purpose. For property management fees paid to a spouse, partner or other relative, the situation will be much the same as in Dama's case in the example set out above.

Whichever type of entity is used, there are two words of warning which we must emphasise:

i)   The management fees charged must not exceed a normal commercial rate and should not exceed the rate charged to other, unconnected, clients (they can be less, however).

ii)   If the total management fees (from all sources) received by the entity in any twelve month period exceed the VAT registration threshold (currently £85,000), he/she/it will need to register for VAT and charge 20% on their fees. This will generally eliminate most, if not all, of any advantage gained through the arrangement.

Look After the Little Things

There are a number of tax deductible items which often get overlooked. For landlords with a marginal tax rate of just 20%, it may seem unnecessarily complex or burdensome to worry about these things when the potential tax savings are small.

However, with many landlords' marginal tax rates increasing to 40% or more from 2017/18 onwards, it may perhaps be a good idea to review some of these items. It is not a case of spending any more money, merely a case of being more meticulous about claiming the expenditure which you are already incurring.

Some of the things we would recommend that you consider are:

- Use of home (even the most minor business use of your own home will generally entitle you to claim an annual deduction of £104; much bigger claims are often justifiable in many cases)

- Motor expenses (are you recording and claiming for all of your business journeys?)

- Capital allowances on equipment and cars (see Chapter 12 for more information)

- Travel and subsistence costs

- Telephone, broadband and other IT expenses

More information on all of these types of expenditure, and on how much you are entitled to claim, is provided in the Taxcafe.co.uk guide *'How to Save Property Tax'*.

Self-Employed Business Owners

Finally, it's worth pointing out again that if you own another unincorporated business, over and above your residential property business, you will have even more flexibility when it comes to increasing your tax deductible expenses in order to save tax.

For example, it may be easier to employ family members in your other business than in your property business.

Increasing tax deductible spending on either business will achieve exactly the same result, which is to reduce your taxable income when the tax relief on your mortgage interest is reduced.

Chapter 14

Accelerating Finance Costs

In Chapter 12, we looked at the potential benefits of postponing tax deductible expenditure so that it falls into a tax year in which you have a higher marginal tax rate.

For finance costs it will often be worth doing the opposite because by 2020/21 these costs will only attract tax relief at 20%. For a typical higher-rate taxpayer with a marginal tax rate of 40%, the effective rate of relief for their finance costs over the next few years will generally be as follows:

2017/18:   35%
2018/19:   30%
2019/20:   25%
2020/21:   20%

For an additional rate taxpayer with a marginal tax rate of 45%, the effective rate of relief will be:

2017/18:   38.75%
2018/19:   32.5%
2019/20:   26.25%
2020/21:   20%

Hence, in short, for both higher and additional rate taxpayers, accelerating finance costs will save tax.

Interest is a time-based cost, so it will seldom be possible for it to be accelerated. (Unless someone starts offering reduced interest rates for years three and four of a mortgage instead of years one and two: or something similar.)

But there might be opportunities to accelerate other finance costs.

For a start, there is the simple fact that loan arrangement fees and other costs associated with obtaining a mortgage or long-term loan must generally be claimed over the **useful** life of that loan. Many landlords, however, claim these costs over the **legal** life of the loan.

Example

Omar is a higher-rate taxpayer. On 6th April 2016, he took out an interest only buy-to-let mortgage with a 20 year term. He incurred a loan arrangement fee and various other related costs totalling £2,000.

Before reading this guide, he was planning to claim these costs over 20 years, i.e. £100 per year, despite the fact that he fully intends to remortgage in 2021/22, just after the initial five year period (with a reduced interest rate) has expired.

Following this method, Omar would end up claiming £100 in each year from 2016/17 to 2020/21 and the balance of £1,500 in 2021/22. The total value of his tax relief would be £450 (£40 + £35 + £30 + £25 + £20 + £1,500 x 20%).

However, having read this guide (and being surprised to find himself in it), Omar realises that he may legitimately claim these costs over the five year period from 2016/17 to 2020/21, i.e. at £400 per year. This produces tax relief with a total value of £600 (£160 + £140 + £120 + £100 + £80).

Not only does Omar obtain tax relief much earlier, he also enjoys an overall additional saving of £150.

When claiming loan arrangement fees and other associated costs over a shorter period than the legal life of the loan, it is essential to record and retain evidence of your logic for doing so: i.e. the reasons why you believe that the **useful** life of the loan is shorter than the **legal** life of the loan.

How About Remortgaging Sooner?

It may even be worth actually changing your plans in order to accelerate finance costs which you know you are going to incur so that they arise earlier.

If there is no additional cost in doing this then it will generally be worthwhile, but it may even sometimes be worth incurring a small additional cost.

Example

Toshiko is an additional rate taxpayer. She has a 10 year commercial loan over her residential property portfolio which is due to expire in May 2022. She is currently claiming the initial loan arrangement fee and other associated costs over the ten year life of the loan at £2,000 per year.

Toshiko expects the costs of refinancing her portfolio to amount to £25,000. If she does this before 2022, there will be an early repayment penalty of £1,250.

We will assume for the sake of illustration that Toshiko will claim the costs of her new loan over an expected useful life of ten years.

If Toshiko waits until 2022 to remortgage her property, she will obtain tax relief as follows:

2017/18:	*£2,000 x 38.75% =*	*£775*
2018/19:	*£2,000 x 32.5% =*	*£650*
2019/20:	*£2,000 x 26.25% =*	*£525*
2020/21:	*£2,000 x 20% =*	*£400*
2021/22:	*£2,000 x 20% =*	*£400*
2022/23 & later:	*£25,000 x 20% =*	*£5,000*
Total Relief:		*£7,750*

Instead, however, Toshiko refinances her portfolio during 2017/18. This gives her costs of £13,750 to claim straight away: the remaining £10,000 of costs on her old loan, the £1,250 early repayment penalty, and the first of ten claims at £2,500 per year in respect of the new loan. She will also be able to claim £2,500 per year for the next nine years. This provides tax relief as follows:

2017/18:	*£13,750 x 38.75% =*	*£5,328*
2018/19:	*£2,500 x 32.5% =*	*£813*
2019/20:	*£2,500 x 26.25% =*	*£656*
2020/21 & later:	*£17,500 x 20% =*	*£3,500*
Total Relief:		*£10,297*

The total value of Toshiko's tax relief is increased by £2,547 and, even after accounting for the additional cost of £1,250 (the early repayment penalty) she is still left £1,297 better off overall.

Naturally, there are many other factors which should be considered in a case like this: not least the fact that costs of

£25,000 have been incurred over four years earlier than necessary and also the fact that the new loan may now expire earlier than would otherwise have been the case.

Nevertheless, the example does illustrate the fact that accelerating finance costs may lead to overall savings.

For full details of the treatment of loan arrangement fees and other items which may be claimed as costs of raising long-term finance, as well as the rules for claiming these costs over the useful life of the relevant loan, see the Taxcafe.co.uk guide *'How to Save Property Tax'*.

Accelerating Finance Costs under the Cash Basis

From 6th April 2017, many unincorporated property businesses (i.e. individual landlords) can use the 'cash basis' to calculate their tax.

Landlords who decide to use the cash basis will generally be able to claim all their finance costs (including loan arrangement fees) *as they are paid*, subject to the tax relief restriction which is the focus of this guide.

See Chapter 27 for more information.

Chapter 15

Pension Contributions

A simple way for landlords to beat the tax increase is by upping their pension contributions. How much extra will you need to invest to claw back all the extra tax you will pay? As a rule of thumb, your *gross* pension contribution will need to be half as big as your non-deductible interest. So if you have £10,000 of buy-to-let interest in 2020/21, you'll typically need to make a gross pension contribution of £5,000 to recover the extra tax you'll pay.

Example – Before Pension Contribution

Let's say it's 2020/21 and Usman earns £40,000 as a self-employed consultant and a rental profit of £10,000 (after deducting £10,000 of buy-to-let interest) from some residential properties. If Usman's mortgage tax relief was NOT restricted he would have total taxable income of £50,000 and his total after-tax income would be:

£50,000 income - £7,500 tax = £42,500

However, with his mortgage interest no longer tax deductible, Usman's Income Tax bill will increase by £2,000 to £9,500 (he'll have an extra £10,000 taxed at 40% but will also be entitled to a 20% tax reduction). In summary, his after-tax income will fall from £42,500 to £40,500.

(Usman's National Insurance has been ignored for simplicity.)

Example – After Pension Contribution

Usman decides to invest £4,000 in his pension. The taxman will add £1,000 of basic-rate tax relief, giving him a gross pension contribution of £5,000. He will also receive higher-rate tax relief through his self-assessment tax computation. This is calculated as 20% of his gross pension contribution: £5,000 x 20% = £1,000.

In total Usman enjoys £2,000 tax relief by making a £5,000 gross pension contribution (a cash contribution of £4,000). Hence, all the extra tax arising due to the reduction in his interest relief is clawed back by making a gross pension contribution half as big as his mortgage interest payments.

Pensions: Cashflow Issues

Although you can completely reverse the tax increase by making pension contributions, there is one significant problem: your money is locked away until you reach the minimum retirement age (currently 55). In other words, pension contributions can seriously damage your cashflow!

We saw that Usman's disposable income will fall from £42,500 to £40,500 when his mortgage tax relief is fully restricted. By making a pension contribution he claws back £2,000 and ends up with £42,500 again BUT £5,000 of that is stuck inside a pension plan! His actual disposable income will fall by a further £3,000 to £37,500. Usman's financial position is summarised below:

Usman: Tax Relief versus Cash Flow

	No Pension Contribution	Pension Contribution
	£	£
Self-employment income	40,000	40,000
Taxable rental profit	20,000	20,000
	---------	---------
	60,000	60,000
Less:		
Income tax	9,500[1]	8,500[2]
Pension contribution	0	4,000
Mortgage interest[3]	10,000	10,000
Disposable income[4]	**40,500**	**37,500**
Pension Pot	**0**	**5,000**

Notes
1. First £12,500 tax free, next £37,500 taxed at 20%, final £10,000 taxed at 40%. Reduced by £2,000 tax reduction (mortgage interest x 20%).
2. Further reduced by £1,000 higher-rate tax relief on pension contribution.
3. Taxable rental profit is not the same as actual rental profit; his £10,000 of mortgage interest must be deducted to calculate his true disposable income.
4. Ignores National Insurance payments. These would be the same under both scenarios and hence do not alter the overall conclusion.

Why does Usman's disposable income fall by £3,000? Because he personally invests £4,000 into his pension but gets £1,000 of higher-rate tax relief back through his self-assessment tax computation.

In summary, when we get to 2020/21, for every £10,000 of mortgage interest you pay you will generally be able to claw back the extra tax you will face as a higher-rate taxpayer by making a £5,000 gross pension contribution. £3,000 will ultimately come from you and £2,000 from the taxman. Thus, your disposable income will also fall by a further £3,000.

Pension Contributions this Year (2017/18)

What about the current 2017/18 tax year? By how much do you have to increase your pension contributions to reverse the tax increase you will suffer now that one quarter of your interest is no longer tax deductible?

Example
Let's assume that in 2017/18 Usman has the same income and expenses as in the previous examples. With one quarter (£2,500) of his mortgage interest no longer tax deductible, his taxable income will increase from £50,000 to £52,500. His Income Tax bill will increase by £500 (he'll pay 40% tax on an extra £2,500 but will also be entitled to a 20% tax reduction).

Usman decides to invest £1,000 in his pension. The taxman will add £250 of basic-rate tax relief, giving him a gross pension contribution of £1,250. He will also receive higher-rate tax relief through his self-assessment tax computation. This is calculated as 20% of his gross pension contribution: £1,250 x 20% = £250.

In total, Usman enjoys £500 tax relief by making a £1,250 gross pension contribution (a cash contribution of £1,000).

Just as in the previous example all the extra tax arising due to the reduction in his interest relief is clawed back by making a gross pension contribution half as big as his non-deductible interest.

Once again Usman will have to remember that the money in his pension cannot be touched until he is at least 55.

Protecting Your Child Benefit

So far we've looked at the "bread and butter" case where the landlord is a regular higher-rate taxpayer and enjoys 40% tax relief on their pension contributions. Some landlords may be able to enjoy even more tax relief.

Take Usman, for example. His taxable income rises from £50,000 to £52,500 in 2017/18 and to £60,000 in 2020/21.

With income over £50,000 he will end up paying the child benefit charge if he is a parent and the highest earner in the household. In this case a pension contribution will reduce his "adjusted net income" which will also reduce the child benefit charge.

For example, in 2020/21 his £5,000 gross pension contribution will reduce his adjusted net income from £60,000 to £55,000 which means his child benefit charge will be halved from around £2,500 to £1,250 (if he has three children, based on current rates). In total, Usman will enjoy £3,250 tax relief on his £5,000 pension contribution, i.e. 65% tax relief.

Other Important Tax Thresholds

If your taxable income gets pushed over the £100,000 tax threshold this year you will also start losing your personal allowance. Once your income reaches £123,000 your personal allowance will be completely withdrawn.

However, making pension contributions will reduce your adjusted net income which means you will also recover some of your personal allowance, as well as enjoying the regular pension tax reliefs.

As a result, making pension contributions while your income is in the £100,000-£123,000 tax bracket will generally attract 60% tax relief this year.

If your taxable income gets pushed over the £150,000 tax threshold this year you will start paying additional rate tax at 45%.

However, making pension contributions to claw back the extra tax is more difficult for high income earners.

Since 6th April 2016 the annual allowance (the maximum amount you can invest each year in a pension) has been reduced for those with "adjusted income" in excess of £150,000.

Broadly speaking, your adjusted income is your total taxable income plus any pension contributions made by your employer and any pension contributions made under a net pay arrangement (where your pension contributions are made by means of payroll deduction).

If your adjusted income exceeds £150,000, your annual allowance will be gradually reduced from £40,000 to £10,000. £1 of allowance will be lost for every additional £2 of income.

As long as your contributions do not exceed the reduced annual allowance you will still receive full tax relief, up to 45%.

(See the Taxcafe.co.uk guide *'Pension Magic'* for further details.)

Postponing Pension Contributions

If you expect to be pushed into a higher tax bracket in a future tax year as the tax relief on your mortgage interest is reduced, should you postpone making any pension contributions so that you can enjoy more tax relief? An obvious example is a basic-rate taxpayer who expects to become a higher-rate taxpayer when less of their interest is tax deductible.

Example
During the current 2017/18 tax year Oswald has net rental income of £40,000 (after deducting his various costs except interest). His total interest payments are £20,000. He also has other taxable earnings of £20,000.

One quarter of his mortgage interest (£5,000) is no longer tax deductible so his taxable income will be £45,000 (£40,000 rental income - £15,000 interest + £20,000 other income).

Oswald will not be a higher-rate taxpayer in 2017/18 because his taxable income does not exceed the higher rate tax threshold of £45,000. If he makes any pension contributions in 2017/18 he will only enjoy basic-rate tax relief.

Now let's move forward to the 2020/21 tax year (when none of his mortgage interest will be tax deductible and the higher-rate threshold is expected to be £50,000). Oswald will now have taxable income of £60,000 which means he'll have £10,000 taxed at 40%.

This also means that if he makes a gross pension contribution of £10,000 he will enjoy 40% tax relief. If his household also receives child benefit then the pension contribution will also ensure that he does not pay the child benefit charge as well (assuming he is the highest earner in the household).

Should landlords postpone making pension contributions and build up some savings to make bigger than normal pension contributions several years from now when they will possibly enjoy at least twice as much tax relief?

In an ideal world the answer would be yes. However, with tax rules constantly changing there is no guarantee that you will enjoy more tax relief on your pension contributions in the future.

Many pension experts believe that higher-rate tax relief will eventually be abolished (apparently the Government wanted to do this before the EU referendum but backed down). If higher-rate tax relief will be abolished then higher-rate taxpayers should make the most of the existing rules while they can.

Basic-rate taxpayers arguably face less risk by postponing pension contributions until they become higher-rate taxpayers because any change is less likely to leave them worse off.

However, pension contributions should arguably never be postponed if this also means giving up contributions from your employer (which are essentially additional pay in a tax efficient form).

It's also important to point out that, since 6th April 2017, a new type of savings product has been available: the Lifetime ISA. Lifetime ISAs are open to those under age 40 and offer a 25% Government bonus on a maximum investment of £4,000 per year.

The Lifetime ISA can be used to save for a first home or for retirement. For basic-rate taxpayers saving for retirement a Lifetime ISA is more tax efficient than a pension. Although both offer the same 25% Government bonus, qualifying withdrawals from the Lifetime ISA will be tax free, whereas pension withdrawals are fully taxed (apart from the 25% tax-free lump sum).

If you are a higher-rate taxpayer a pension will continue to be the more powerful tax shelter if you expect to become a basic-rate taxpayer when you retire (most retirees are basic-rate taxpayers).

Pension Contributions – Other Issues

When it comes to making pension contributions there are lots of things you need to remember, including:

- **Do you have earnings?** Everyone under 75 can make a gross pension contribution of up to £3,600 per year. If you want to contribute more your gross contributions must not exceed your annual earnings. Salaries and trading profits are earnings for this purpose; rental profits generally are not. If you want to make big pension contributions you must have earnings from other sources.

- **The £40,000 Annual Allowance.** Total pension contributions by you and your employer must generally not exceed £40,000 per year, although you can sometimes carry forward unused allowance from earlier tax years.

- **The Lifetime Allowance.** Additional restrictions apply where the total value of all your pension schemes, including the value of any benefits under schemes run by your employer, exceeds the lifetime allowance. This allowance fell to £1m on 6th April 2016.

- **Is Tax Only Deferred and Not Saved?** Subject to the 25% tax-free lump sum, withdrawals from your pension scheme will be taxable. Arguably, therefore, your pension contributions are only deferring tax rather than saving it. However, much of this depends on how you time your withdrawals and on what your income situation is at the time; so absolute savings are still possible if you get your timing right!

(This is just a brief overview. For more information see the Taxcafe.co.uk guide *'Pension Magic'*.)

Chapter 16

Should You Reduce Your Buy-to-Let Mortgages?

Many landlords are wondering whether they should reduce their mortgages as the tax relief on their interest is reduced.

However, reducing your buy-to-let debt will not solve the fundamental problem you may face thanks to this tax change: being pushed into a higher tax bracket and paying tax on rental profits that don't really exist.

Paying down debt may actually *increase* your tax bill, not reduce it – if your interest payments get smaller, your 20% basic-rate tax reduction will also get smaller.

Paying down debt may, nevertheless, lead to an increase in your after-tax disposable income if you can't get a better return elsewhere on your surplus cash. There are, of course, other things you can do with your surplus cash including:

- Keep it in a tax-free savings account
- Pay down other debts (e.g. the mortgage on your home)
- Use it to fund further property purchases

If your savings are kept in an ISA the interest will, of course, be tax free. Furthermore, since 2016/17 a new personal savings allowance has been available which exempts the first £1,000 of interest you earn from tax if you are a basic-rate taxpayer (£500 if you are a higher-rate taxpayer).

Even though it may be tax free, the interest you can earn on your savings is usually lower than the interest you pay on your borrowings, so you may still be better off using your savings to reduce your debt.

However, many landlords may feel that this could leave them vulnerable. Cash kept in a savings account can be used as a contingency fund to cover repairs and other unforeseen expenses related to your property business.

You could also use your savings to reduce any personal debt you have. Interest rates on credit cards and most short-term borrowings are generally much higher than mortgage rates and usually enjoy no tax relief whatsoever, so it is usually most efficient to pay off these debts first.

If you don't have any short-term borrowings you could use any surplus cash you have to reduce the mortgage on your home, if you have one. Interest rates on buy-to-let mortgages are generally higher than the interest rates on home loans and the product fees are often higher too. So at first glance it would appear that paying off buy-to-let debt is a better idea.

However, because buy-to-let interest enjoys tax relief, you may find that the mortgage on your home is actually more expensive and should be repaid first.

Calculating the Real Cost of Buy-to-Let Interest

Before you pay off any of your buy-to-let debt you should calculate its true after-tax cost. For example, let's say you have a £100,000 buy-to-let mortgage and the interest rate is 3%. Your annual interest bill will be £3,000 but this year (2017/18) you will enjoy £1,050 of tax relief if you are a higher-rate taxpayer:

£3,000 x 75% x 40% = £900
£3,000 x 25% x 20% = £150
Total   £1,050

The true cost of the loan is therefore £1,950, i.e. 1.95%. So if the interest on your personal debt (e.g. the mortgage on your home) is *more than* 1.95% you should pay off your personal debt first. Otherwise you should pay off your buy-to-let mortgage first.

Moving forward to 2020/21, none of your buy-to-let interest will be tax deductible but you will be entitled to a 20% tax reduction of £600 (£3,000 x 20% = £600). The true cost of the loan will then rise to £2,400, i.e. 2.4%.

So if the interest on your personal debt (e.g. the mortgage on your home) is *more than* 2.4% you should pay off that other debt first. Otherwise you should pay off your buy-to-let mortgage first.

Example – 2017/18

In 2017/18 Rees is a higher-rate taxpayer who has £10,000 sitting in a cash ISA earning 1.5% tax free – £150 per year.

He has a mortgage on his home on which he is paying 3% interest. So if he takes his £10,000 of ISA savings and uses it to reduce his home mortgage he will save £300 per year.

He also has a buy-to-let mortgage on which he is paying 4%. If he uses his ISA savings to reduce this debt he will save £400 per year in interest. However, he will also lose £140 in tax relief this year. So his net saving is just £260.

Clearly the best option for Rees this year is to reduce the mortgage on his home. If he didn't have a home mortgage his best bet would be to pay off some of his buy-to-let debt.

Although this may be the "optimal" route to take there may be other reasons why Rees wishes to keep a cash reserve, for example to cover unforeseen expenses. He also needs to consider what the position will be in the future, when his buy-to-let interest relief has been further reduced.

Example – 2020/21

Let's move forward to 2020/21 and assume Rees still has a buy-to-let mortgage on which he is paying 4%. If he uses his £10,000 ISA savings to reduce this debt he will save £400 per year. However, he will also lose £80 of tax relief (£400 x 20%). So his net saving will be £320.

The best option for Rees now is to pay off his buy-to-let debt.

Remember that you may incur early repayment charges when you pay off certain types of mortgage debt. This may affect your decision to repay one debt rather than another.

Chapter 17

Selling Property

It's unlikely many landlords will take the "nuclear option" and sell their properties as their mortgage tax relief is reduced – most, we suspect, will simply take the tax hit on the chin.

For most landlords, investing in property will become less profitable but not necessarily *unprofitable* – many will probably continue to enjoy a positive rental profit (unless interest rates increase significantly) and will probably still see property as the best way to accumulate wealth.

Remember returns from property come in two flavours: rental income and capital growth. Many landlords will be willing to pay more Income Tax if they're enjoying an even higher amount of capital growth.

Even if property prices increase by just one or two per cent per year many landlords will still end up better off overall, despite the loss of some of their tax relief. Of course capital growth is not guaranteed and property prices can and do fall.

Unfortunately not all landlords are in such a happy situation. Some, in particular those with large portfolios with lots of debt, may suffer such a sharp decline in income they may be forced to sell up. Before we take a look at a few examples, let's remind ourselves how Capital Gains Tax is calculated.

Capital Gains Tax Basics

If you sell a rental property you could end up paying Capital Gains Tax. For a full discussion of this complex tax we recommend reading the Taxcafe.co.uk guide *'How to Save Property Tax'*.

Essentially you pay Capital Gains Tax on your profit which is generally the difference between the price you paid for the property and the price you sell it for. You can also deduct your buying and selling costs from your profit, typically Stamp Duty Land Tax, estate agent fees and legal fees. You can also deduct the cost of any improvements you have made to the property (but not repairs – see Chapter 12). Finally, you can deduct the Capital Gains Tax annual exemption (currently £11,300).

This leaves you with your taxable gain which is taxed at 28% if you are a higher-rate taxpayer and 18% to the extent your basic-rate band is not used up by your income. For most assets these Capital Gains Tax rates were reduced to 20% and 10% respectively from 6th April 2016 but NOT for residential property.

Those thinking of selling properties may wish to consider selling those that have the smallest capital gains, although, naturally, there are lots of other factors that may affect this decision.

Landlord Suffers Rental Loss

One group of landlords who may decide to scale back their portfolios are those who don't depend on their properties for rental income but, thanks to the interest tax change, end up making rental losses on some of their properties.

Example
Anna is a higher-rate taxpayer who works full-time and also owns two rental properties. She doesn't rely on the properties for income but isn't prepared to accept rental losses ("Investments aren't supposed to lose you money, especially when they take up so much of your time").

The first property was purchased many years ago for £100,000 and is now worth £200,000. The second property was purchased recently in the same area for £200,000, using a £150,000 buy-to-let mortgage and by borrowing £50,000 against her first property.

Let's say she receives net rental income of £10,000 per year from the second property. This is after deducting all her costs except mortgage interest which comes to £8,000 per year. With a taxable rental profit of £2,000 she paid £800 Income Tax last year (2016/17), leaving her with an after-tax rental profit of £1,200 on this property.

Assuming rent and interest rates remain the same, the after-tax rental profit on the second property falls to £800 in 2017/18, £400 in 2018/19, £0 in 2019/20 and she'll incur a loss of £400 in 2020/21. Her after-tax profits fall as the tax relief on her mortgage interest is gradually reduced.

Because Anna is making a rental loss, in the absence of any increase in the rent she can charge, she must rely on capital growth to make the investment worthwhile.

Fortunately, even if the property only increases in value by one or two per cent per year this will more than compensate for her £400 rental loss. For example, if the property rises by just two per cent per year she will enjoy an annual capital gain of at least £4,000.

Of course, capital gains are by no means guaranteed and the property could fall in value.

If Anna decides to sell the property in 2020/21 and receives more than £200,000 for it, she may be subject to Capital Gains Tax. For example, let's assume that after deducting all of her buying and selling costs, she is left with a gain of £30,000.

If the annual Capital Gains Tax exemption has risen to £12,000 by then, this will leave her with a taxable gain of £18,000 and a tax bill of £5,040 (£18,000 x 28%).

Anna sells the property to stem her rental loss, but the Capital Gains Tax bill is more than 12 times bigger than her annual rental loss!

Clearly, deciding whether a property should be sold is a complex matter and would need to be based on many factors – not just a rental loss in one year. Anna will need to think about where she sees rents, interest rates and property prices going in the years ahead. Unfortunately all of these are impossible to predict!

Nevertheless, many landlords who end up with modest rental losses may decide to hold onto their properties because, being an optimistic bunch, most believe rents and capital values will continue to rise over the long term.

Landlord Suffers Huge Drop in Income

Those most likely to sell are landlords who depend on their properties for income AND see their income fall sharply when their mortgage tax relief is reduced. Those most at risk of this happening are landlords who have big property portfolios but also large amounts of debt.

Example

Remember Katerina from Case Study 6 in Chapter 6 who owns the heavily geared property portfolio? In 2020/21, with her interest no longer tax deductible, her taxable rental profit will rise from £50,000 to £125,000. Not only will she end up paying tax at 40% she will also lose her child benefit and Income Tax personal allowance. As a result her after-tax income will fall from £45,000 to £22,500 – a drop of 50%!

Katerina can no longer pay the household bills and decides to sell 60% of her properties. As a result her taxable income will also fall by 60% from £125,000 back to £50,000. She will no longer be subject to 40% tax and will keep all of her child benefit and Income Tax personal allowance. The first £12,500 of her income will be tax free and the remainder will be taxed at 20%, giving her a tax bill of £7,500.

What about her interest payments? Let's assume her portfolio is worth around £2.67 million and she has 75% buy-to-let mortgages totalling £2 million. This means her total equity is around £670,000.

To give Katerina the best outcome possible we'll assume she does not have to pay any Capital Gains Tax on the properties she sells – we'll assume they've barely risen in value since she bought them.

If she sells 60% of her properties her debt will fall by 60% from £2 million to £800,000. Furthermore, she will also release 60% of her equity (roughly £400,000) which can also be used to reduce the debt on her remaining properties. As a result her total debt will fall by 80% to £400,000 which means her interest payments will also fall by 80% from £75,000 to £15,000.

Her interest payments will not be tax deductible but she will be entitled to a 20% tax reduction which amounts to £3,000, giving her a final Income Tax bill of £4,500.

Katerina's after-tax disposable income is calculated as follows:

	£
Net rental income	50,000
Child benefit	2,500
Less: Interest	15,000
Less: Tax	4,500
After-tax income	33,000

By selling 60% of her properties, Katerina has managed to increase her after-tax income by over £10,000: from £22,500 to £33,000!

However, she's still £12,000 short of the £45,000 she would have made if her interest payments were fully tax deductible. Furthermore, she will also lose out on a lot of capital growth if the properties she sold would have risen in value in the years ahead.

To cover the £12,000 black hole in her income Katerina may need to find a part-time job or start another business. Hopefully with a much smaller property portfolio she will have more time on her hands to do this!

Chapter 18

Company Owners with Dividend Income

Landlords who also own their own companies should consider paying themselves more dividend income this year if they expect their marginal tax rate to increase in the future.

This is one of the main tax benefits of being a company owner. Unlike regular salaried employees or owners of unincorporated businesses (e.g. sole traders), company owners can control the amount of income they receive and therefore control their personal Income Tax bills.

Many company owners pay themselves a small tax-free salary and take the rest of their income as dividends (because there is no National Insurance on dividends).

The first £5,000 of dividend income you receive in 2017/18 is tax free thanks to the "dividend allowance". All taxpayers, regardless of income, receive this allowance. Unfortunately, the dividend allowance is expected to be reduced to £2,000 in 2018/19.

For those receiving dividends in excess of the dividend allowance, the following Income Tax rates apply:

Basic-rate taxpayers   7.5%
Higher-rate taxpayers   32.5%
Additional-rate taxpayers   38.1%

Dividends are always treated as the top slice of your income and are therefore subject to the highest possible tax rate.

Company owners who are also landlords should consider paying themselves as much dividend income as they can taxed at 7.5% over the next few years if they think the mortgage tax relief restriction will force them to pay 32.5% tax in the future.

This year company owners will generally start paying 32.5% tax on their dividends once their total taxable income exceeds £45,000.

Example

Jessie owns a small engineering company and pays herself a salary of £11,500 which is tax free thanks to her personal allowance (ignoring a small amount of National Insurance). She also owns a couple of rental properties and earns net rental income of £24,000 and pays £14,000 interest on her buy-to-let mortgages. To keep things simple we'll assume her rental income and expenses stay the same for the next few years.

During the current 2017/18 tax year three quarters of her finance costs are tax deductible so she will have a taxable rental profit of £13,500. This means she can pay herself a dividend of up to £20,000 before she becomes a higher-rate taxpayer and has to pay 32.5% tax (£45,000 - £11,500 - £13,500). The first £5,000 will be tax free and the remainder will be taxed at 7.5%.

By the time we get to 2020/21 the personal allowance and higher-rate threshold are expected to be at least £12,500 and £50,000 respectively. None of Jessie's finance costs will be tax deductible so she will have a taxable rental profit of £24,000. Assuming she pays herself a salary of £12,500, this means she can pay herself a dividend of up to £13,500 before she becomes a higher-rate taxpayer and has to pay 32.5% tax (£50,000 - £12,500 - £24,000).

In summary, the maximum amount of dividend income Jessie can extract from her company taxed at no more than 7.5% is £20,000 this year and will gradually fall to £13,500 in 2020/21. She should consider paying herself these "maximum amounts" between now and 2020/21, even though she may not need the income immediately.

Other Important Tax Thresholds

If her company has enough profits to distribute, Jessie may decide to pay herself a dividend of more than £20,000 this year, even though she will have to pay 32.5% tax on the additional income.

She may decide to do this if she thinks her company will make decent profits in the future and her taxable income may rise above £50,000. At that point she could be subject to the child benefit charge if she has young children and is the highest earner in the household.

For the highest earner in the household the child benefit charge creates the following marginal tax rates on dividend income in the £50,000-£60,000 tax bracket:

Children	Marginal Tax Rate on Dividends
1	43%
2	50%
3	58%
4	65%

Plus 7% for each additional child

Income under £100,000

Company owners with income under £100,000 may wish to consider upping their dividends (where profits allow) if they think their taxable income will rise above £100,000 as the tax relief on their mortgage interest is further reduced.

Once your income rises above £100,000, your personal allowance is gradually withdrawn. At this point you could end up paying Income Tax at an effective rate of over 50% on some of your dividend income. So paying 32.5% now may be preferable, even if you do not need the income immediately.

Distributable Profits

As mentioned once or twice above, companies may only pay dividends to the extent that they have distributable profits available, as evidenced by a suitable set of accounts. Gains arising on property revaluations do not represent distributable profits for this purpose.

For more information on the limitations and formalities applying to the payment of dividends, see the Taxcafe.co.uk guide *'Using a Property Company to Save Tax'*.

Chapter 19

Emigration

If you decide to retire or work abroad you will still have to pay UK Income Tax on your rental properties situated in the UK. However, once you become non-resident it's possible the reduction in interest tax relief will affect you much less or not at all. This will typically be the case if the only UK income you have is from UK properties.

Example – UK Resident
To keep things simple we'll assume it's the 2020/21 tax year (when the mortgage tax relief restriction will have full force). Dennis is a UK resident with a salary of £60,000. He also has rental income of £40,000 and property expenses of £6,000, so his taxable rental profit is £34,000. He also pays £14,000 in mortgage interest but none of this is deductible when calculating his taxable rental profit.

With this much salary Dennis is a higher-rate taxpayer and will pay 40% tax on the £34,000 taxable rental profit – £13,600. He will also receive a tax reduction equal to 20% of his interest – £2,800. Thus in total he pays £10,800 tax on his rental income.

Example revised – Non-Resident
This time we will assume Dennis is non-resident. He still earns a salary of £60,000 but none of this is taxable in the UK. With no other UK income the first £12,500 of his £34,000 taxable rental profit will be tax free (the Government has promised to increase the personal allowance to at least £12,500 by 2020/21). Income Tax at 20% will be payable on the remainder – £4,300. He will also enjoy a tax reduction equal to 20% of his mortgage interest – £2,800. In total he pays £1,500 Income Tax on his rental income.

As a non-resident, Dennis will pay £9,300 less UK tax on his rental income. With no other UK income, some of his rental income is tax free thanks to his personal allowance and the rest is taxed at just 20%. As a basic-rate taxpayer Dennis is completely unaffected by the mortgage tax relief restriction. Even though his interest is no longer a tax deductible expense, none of his income is pushed into the 40% tax bracket.

The 20% tax he pays on some of his rental income (because his interest costs are not deductible) is completely offset by an identical 20% tax reduction.

Other Issues for Non-Residents

Other UK Income
Non-residents who have other UK income, apart from their rental income, are more likely to be affected by the reduction in interest tax relief.

As a non-resident there is no UK tax payable on salary you receive for doing work outside the UK. However, you could still be subject to UK tax for duties performed in the UK, unless they are "merely incidental" to your overseas job.

If you retire abroad you will probably receive a UK pension. Under the terms of many of the UK's double tax treaties, only the country where you live can tax your pension. Thus many retirees do not pay any UK tax on their UK pensions. Government pensions are an exception. Tax is usually only payable in the UK, with no tax payable overseas. Note that every double tax agreement has different terms, so you will need to do a bit of research before you emigrate.

Some countries don't have a double tax agreement with the UK and in these cases your pension will remain taxable in the UK.

Personal Allowance
Not all non-residents are entitled to a personal allowance to set against their UK rental (or other) income. The normal personal allowance (£11,500 for 2017/18) is, however, currently available to:

- British nationals resident abroad
- Nationals of other states within the European Economic Area
- Crown servants
- Residents of the Isle of Man
- Residents of the Channel Islands
- Residents of countries which have a suitable double taxation agreement with the UK

Capital Gains Tax

Emigration may not only help you reduce your UK Income Tax, it may also help you pay less Capital Gains Tax.

Non-residents are no longer completely exempt from Capital Gains Tax when they sell UK residential property. However, only gains that have arisen since 6th April 2015 are taxable.

Gains that arose before this date are completely free from UK tax, providing you remain non-resident for more than five years.

Overseas Tax

Your UK rental income may also be taxable in the country where you are now resident for tax purposes. If this is the case, any UK tax you pay will probably be allowed as a credit against your overseas tax bill.

Some countries are more generous than others and offer concessions to new residents such as a tax exemption for their overseas (i.e. UK) income. Australia is one such country.

Mortgage Issues

Becoming non-resident could affect your ability to take out new mortgages or remortgage existing properties because only a small proportion of buy-to-let lenders currently offer their products to expats.

For example, if your existing fixed-rate deals come to an end while you are non-resident, you could be stuck paying the lender's standard variable rate (or other "revert to" rate) unless you can find new fixed-rate deals from another lender who is willing to deal with expats.

Chapter 20

Investing in Different Types of Property

As explained in Chapter 3, the interest relief restrictions do not apply to funds borrowed for investment in non-residential property, or in qualifying furnished holiday lettings.

As far as future investments are concerned, it would be a relatively simple matter for an investor to change their strategy and begin building a portfolio of either commercial property (shops, offices, pubs, restaurants, etc) or furnished holiday lettings.

Managing these investments does require a different 'skill set', however, and this is something which a residential landlord should bear in mind. Furthermore, a property can only qualify as a furnished holiday let if certain strict criteria are met (see the Taxcafe.co.uk guide *'How to Save Property Tax'* for details).

Converting Existing Property

In some cases, it may be possible to convert existing property to either commercial use or to a furnished holiday let.

A city-centre ground floor flat might be suitable for converting into a cafe; the upper storeys of the same building might be suitable for furnished holiday letting; or the whole property might make a good office building.

Rural properties may often lend themselves to furnished holiday letting too.

All of this depends on the type of property, its location, and on obtaining the necessary permission for 'change of use'. Not all properties will be suitable, but it may be worth considering the idea in some cases.

Better Borrowing

In some cases, there may be scope to effectively arrange your borrowings so that more of them relate to non-residential property or furnished holiday lettings.

The simple idea of mortgaging a commercial property or furnished holiday let and using the funds to pay off the mortgage on a residential property will not work, however, as the new borrowings will clearly have been invested in residential property.

However, let us suppose that you have £100,000 of available cash (e.g. from the sale of a rental property) and you use this to pay off the mortgage on a residential property.

Then, a year or two later, you might invest in a commercial property or a furnished holiday let. You could borrow against the new property, or indeed any other property, use the funds for your investment and retain full tax relief on the interest arising (plus the loan arrangement fees and other associated costs).

If, instead, you had simply used the £100,000 of cash to purchase your new investment, you would have been left with a mortgage on a residential property with interest relief restricted to basic rate only.

Overseas Property

Interest on borrowings used to finance purchases of overseas residential property will be subject to the same restrictions as for purchases of UK residential property.

There are therefore only two ways in which investing in overseas residential property might help with your interest relief restriction:

i)   Property in the European Economic Area which is used as a furnished holiday let will be exempt from the interest relief restriction

ii)   If you were to emigrate and become non-UK resident at some stage in the future, you would cease to be subject to UK Income Tax on rental income from overseas property

When investing in overseas property, it is essential to bear in mind that you may be subject to tax in the country in which the property is located. Those who emigrate will also generally be subject to tax in the country in which they are resident for tax purposes.

Chapter 21

Alternative Investment Structures

Higher-rate taxpayers who wish to make new property investments may now wish to consider using alternative investment structures in order to avoid the problem of being taxed on profits that they will not receive if they were to use the traditional buy-to-let mortgage model.

Shared Equity

Rather than borrow the funds required to make a purchase, it may be possible to enter into a shared equity arrangement whereby the property is effectively shared with another party.

Example
Morgan is a higher rate taxpayer. She wishes to purchase a residential property valued at £100,000 but has only £75,000 available to invest. The property will produce a rental profit (after all expenses except interest) of £5,000. If Morgan borrows the additional £25,000 which she needs, she will incur an annual interest cost of £1,000. Under the regime applying from 2020/21 onwards, her net tax liability on the income from the property would be £1,800 (£5,000 x 40% less £1,000 x 20%), leaving her with after tax income of £2,200.

Instead, Morgan enters into a shared equity arrangement whereby she purchases a 75% share of the property for £75,000 and another party acquires a 25% share of the property. It is agreed that Morgan will receive 80% of the net rental profit: her increased share reflecting the fact that she will be managing the property.

Morgan now has a rental profit of £4,000 (£5,000 x 80%), a tax liability of £1,600 (£4,000 x 40%), and is left with after tax income of £2,400: i.e. £200 more than if she had taken out a mortgage.

This strategy would be even more worthwhile for a landlord with a marginal tax rate greater than 40%.

The downside is that Morgan will be losing out on 25% of the property's capital growth.

Syndicates

Another way to invest in property without borrowing is to invest via a syndicate.

For example, four additional rate taxpayer individuals could each invest £50,000 in a residential rental property and would each receive rental profits of, say, £2,500, leaving each of them with after tax income of £1,375 (after tax at 45%).

If, instead, each had gone out and borrowed £150,000 at 4% and bought their own £200,000 property, then each would receive rental profits of £10,000 taxed at 45% (£4,500), and pay interest of £6,000 which would attract tax relief at just 20% (£1,200). Each investor's after tax income would then be just £700 (£10,000 - £4,500 - £6,000 + £1,200).

Using the syndicate almost doubles each investor's return!

The downside, once again, is that each investor is enjoying less capital growth: only a quarter share in this case in fact.

Note
Using the same figures for higher-rate taxpayers with a marginal tax rate of 40% produces after tax income of £1,500 each using a syndicate compared with £1,200 using a buy-to-let mortgage. Not quite as beneficial, but still better overall (from an income perspective only).

Chapter 22

Transferring Property to Your Spouse or Partner

Making sure properties are owned by the spouse with the lowest tax rate is a well-known tax saving technique. This strategy may become even more popular as tax relief on mortgage interest is further reduced.

Example – 2017/18 Tax Year
Shakeel is a higher-rate taxpayer with self-employment income of £50,000 from a small shop. He also owns a residential property that generates net rental income of £10,000 and pays £5,000 interest on his buy-to-let mortgage. With three quarters of his interest tax deductible this year his taxable rental profit will be £6,250. He'll pay 40% tax (£2,500) but will also be entitled to a tax reduction equal to 20% of the disallowed mortgage interest (£250), so his total tax bill on the rental income will be £2,250.

Shakeel's wife Nazreen earns a salary of £20,000 and is a basic-rate taxpayer. If Nazreen owns the property she'll pay 20% tax on the £6,250 rental profit (£1,250) but will also be entitled to a 20% tax reduction (£250), so her total tax bill on the rental income will be £1,000.

The couple will save £1,250 if Nazreen owns the property.

Example – 2020/21 Tax Year
If Shakeel owns the property in 2020/21 he will have a taxable rental profit of £10,000. He'll pay 40% tax (£4,000) but will also be entitled to a 20% tax reduction (£1,000), so his total tax bill on the rental income will be £3,000.

If Nazreen owns the property she will also have a taxable rental profit of £10,000 but will pay just £2,000 tax. She will also be entitled to a £1,000 tax reduction, so her total tax bill on the rental income will still be £1,000 – as a basic-rate taxpayer she is completely unaffected by the change to interest tax relief.

The couple will now save £2,000 if Nazreen owns the property.

Who Can Save Tax?

Tax savings are typically possible when the transferor is a higher-rate taxpayer and the transferee is a basic-rate taxpayer (and remains a basic-rate taxpayer after the transfer).

Additional savings may be possible if the household receives child benefit and, thanks to the transfer, both spouses end up earning less than £60,000 (and preferably no more than £50,000).

For example, if Shakeel owns the property the couple will effectively lose all their child benefit; if Nazreen owns the property they will lose none of it.

It may also be possible to save tax by transferring property if one person ends up with taxable income over £100,000 (personal allowance withdrawn) or £150,000 (additional-rate tax payable).

Future Tax Years

The tax savings enjoyed by transferring property could be short lived. For example, if a property is transferred to a basic-rate taxpayer and that person eventually becomes a higher-rate taxpayer because they begin to receive pension income, or because their salary or other non-property income grows significantly, the tax savings could then be erased completely.

In other words, when deciding what share of a property to transfer to your spouse you should look ahead to future tax years, rather than focus on the tax savings in a single year alone.

Joint Ownership Basics

When a property is already owned jointly by a couple it may be possible to change the ownership split to produce a better tax outcome but there are some traps to watch out for.

In England and Wales there are two types of joint ownership:

- Joint tenancy
- Tenancy in common

With joint tenancy, each joint owner is treated as having an equal share of the property and the income is split 50:50.

With tenancy in common, the shares in the property do not have to be equal. A tenancy in common therefore provides far more scope for tax planning.

In Scotland the most common form of joint ownership is *Pro Indivisio*, which is much the same as a tenancy in common.

It's important to point out that a joint tenancy can be changed to a tenancy in common.

Income Tax Elections

Where a property is held jointly by a married couple, the default Income Tax treatment is a 50:50 split, even if the property is owned in unequal shares.

If you want to be taxed according to your actual beneficial ownership of the property you have to make an election using Form 17 from HM Revenue and Customs. On this form you state the proportions in which the property is owned and this determines how the rental profits are divided for Income Tax purposes.

Such an election will be permanently binding unless the ownership split changes.

Unmarried Couples

A property (or a share in a property) can be transferred from one legally married spouse to another without any Capital Gains Tax charge arising.

With unmarried couples, a transfer from one partner to another or into joint names can result in a Capital Gains Tax charge. The property, or share in the property, which is transferred is taxed as if it had been sold for its market value.

For this reason, it is preferable to get the ownership split right when the property is acquired.

Having said this, joint owners who are not married can agree to split the rental income in a different proportion to their legal ownership of the property.

Hence, for example, an unmarried couple who own a property in equal shares could agree that one person is entitled to 75% of the rental income and the other is entitled to 25%.

It is important to have the income split properly documented in a signed and dated profit-sharing agreement before the start of the tax year, and it is probably advisable to have the income paid into separate bank accounts.

Stamp Duty Land Tax

Stamp Duty Land Tax is probably the biggest cost that could be incurred when a mortgaged property is transferred to a spouse.

Even if your spouse doesn't pay you anything for their share of the property, Stamp Duty Land Tax may be payable if they take on part of the mortgage or other debt over the property.

This is because any debt, or share of debt, which the transferee takes on is effectively deemed to form purchase consideration for Stamp Duty Land Tax purposes: just as if they had paid this amount to acquire the property, or their share of it.

From 1st April 2016 higher rates of Stamp Duty Land Tax are charged on additional residential properties such as buy-to-let properties and second homes.

The new rates are 3% higher than the normal rates:

£0 to £125,000	3%*
£125,000 to £250,000	5%
£250,000 to £925,000	8%
£925,000 to £1.5m	13%
Over £1.5m	15%

*Only applies if total purchase consideration is £40,000 or more. For purchases at less than £40,000, no Stamp Duty Land Tax is payable.

The higher rates will generally apply to a transfer of residential rental property between spouses, based on the amount of mortgage debt effectively taken over by the transferee. For example, if a 50% share of a property with a £200,000 mortgage is transferred from one spouse to another, the Stamp Duty Land Tax bill will usually be £3,000 (£100,000 x 3%).

If a 50% share of a property with a £400,000 mortgage is transferred, the Stamp Duty Land Tax bill will usually be £7,500:

$$£125,000 \times 3\% + £75,000 \times 5\% = £7,500$$

This one-off tax payment will have to be weighed against the potential annual Income Tax saving the couple hope to achieve.

Where two or more residential properties are transferred in a single or linked transaction, something called multiple dwellings relief is available. The rate of Stamp Duty Land Tax is then based on the average purchase consideration (actual or deemed) for each 'dwelling'. The relief is not automatic and must be claimed by the transferee. The extra 3% levy on additional properties continues to apply to the average purchase consideration deemed to be paid.

For example, if the two properties discussed above (one with an outstanding mortgage of £200,000 and one with an outstanding mortgage of £400,000) were both transferred into joint 50/50 ownership with the owner's spouse at the same time, the transferee would be taking on a 50% share of debts totalling £600,000. Hence, they would be deemed to have paid purchase consideration of £300,000. Without multiple dwellings relief, this would usually give rise to Stamp Duty Land Tax of £14,000:

$$£125,000 \times 3\% + £125,000 \times 5\% + £50,000 \times 8\% = £14,000$$

If the transferee claims multiple dwellings relief, the Stamp Duty Land Tax will be based on the average deemed consideration of £150,000 and will then usually amount to £10,000:

$$£125,000 \times 3\% + £25,000 \times 5\% = £5,000 \times 2 = £10,000$$

It is also possible to use the non-residential Stamp Duty Land Tax rates for transfers of six or more dwellings; although the non-residential rates must be applied to the *total* deemed purchase consideration.

Property in Scotland

Purchases or transfers of property located in Scotland are subject to Land and Buildings Transaction Tax and a 3% surcharge also applies to additional residential properties from 1st April 2016:

£0 to £145,000	3%*
£145,000 to £250,000	5%
£250,000 to £325,000	8%
£325,000 to £750,000	13%
Over £750,000	15%

*Only applies if total purchase consideration is £40,000 or more. For purchases at less than £40,000, no Land and Buildings Transaction Tax is payable.

In Scotland, the additional 3% surcharge is known as the 'Additional Dwelling Supplement' and it applies to all purchases or transfers of residential rental property, even if the person acquiring the property has no other interest in any residential property.

As with Stamp Duty Land Tax, any debt, or share of debt, taken on by the transferee is deemed to form purchase consideration for Land and Buildings Transaction Tax purposes.

Multiple dwellings relief generally operates differently under Land and Buildings Transaction Tax. The basic rule remains that the tax is based on the average price of the dwellings being purchased or transferred but, where the Additional Dwelling Supplement applies to any of the properties within the transaction, the Land and Buildings Transaction Tax is calculated separately on each dwelling. This latter method is likely to apply in the vast majority of cases.

Purchases or transfers of six or more dwellings may again alternatively be taxed at non-residential rates: based on the total consideration, or deemed consideration, for the whole transaction.

Property in Wales

Stamp Duty Land Tax will cease to apply to property located in Wales from 1st April 2018, when it will be replaced by Land Transaction Tax, the first devolved tax for Wales.

The rates and bands for Land Transaction Tax are to be announced by 1st October 2017.

Unfortunately, at present, that's all we know. Landlords wishing to transfer property located in Wales therefore have the choice of acting now, under the Stamp Duty Land Tax regime, or waiting to see how the new tax develops. Whether the new tax will lead to savings, or to higher costs, remains to be seen. The experience in Scotland has been savings on lower value properties and higher costs on more valuable properties, but we cannot be certain whether this experience will be replicated in Wales.

Avoiding Stamp Duty Land Tax and Land and Buildings Transaction Tax

The simplest way to avoid paying Stamp Duty Land Tax or Land and Buildings Transaction Tax when a property is transferred to a spouse or partner is to pay off the mortgage first (for example, by remortgaging another property).

Reducing the balance of the mortgage so that the share of debt taken on by the transferee is less than £40,000 will also avoid any Stamp Duty Land Tax or Land and Buildings Transaction Tax charge.

Once the transfer is complete it may be possible to take out a fresh mortgage against the transferred property.

Some landlords may, however, find it difficult to do this sort of juggling act.

Mortgage Issues

One of the biggest potential stumbling blocks when transferring property to your spouse used to be getting permission from the lender, especially if the spouse had only a modest earned income.

However, as the tax rules for buy-to-let properties get increasingly complicated making sure any changes in property ownership don't have unintended consequences is an increasing risk. In particular, if the 3% Stamp Duty Land Tax surcharge is going to be incurred any long term benefits from a change of ownership need to factor in this additional up front cost.

According to Ray Boulger, senior technical manager at mortgage broker John Charcol, if a property is transferred outright from one spouse to another the transferee will have to satisfy the lender's criteria and it would be treated as a new application, thus incurring mortgage fees as well as legal costs.

Most lenders also require the borrower to have a minimum earned income, typically £25,000.

A much better solution, he says, which would allow the mortgage to remain unchanged and incur relatively low legal and mortgage costs, may be to effect a "transfer of equity". This is the process whereby someone is added to the title deeds and requires permission from the lender.

According to Mr Boulger: "Assuming the property is 100% owned it could be transferred into joint ownership on a tenants-in-common basis with, for example, the spouse or partner owning 99% and the original owner 1%."

The mortgage would be on a joint and several liability basis and so the new joint owner would be added to the mortgage with relatively little formality.

Transferring other Assets to Your Spouse

Where transferring a property to your spouse is not possible or is not practical for some reason, it's important to remember that a similar result can often be achieved by transferring other income producing assets.

For example, if you own a company it may be possible to transfer shares to your spouse so that he or she can receive dividends taxed at a lower rate than you.

Chapter 23

Using a Company to Save Tax

Introduction

Interest in using companies to invest in residential property has surged following the announcement that tax relief on finance costs would be reduced for *individual* landlords. Companies are exempt from the change.

Initially, the Government also considered an exemption from the 3% Stamp Duty Land Tax surcharge for companies making "significant" investments in residential property. In the end it was decided that all investors will pay the same Stamp Duty Land Tax. The higher rates apply to all companies purchasing residential property (including their first purchase of a residential property).

There have been a number of important announcements recently that will affect how much tax companies and company owners will pay in future. The Corporation Tax rate will be reduced in the years ahead but Income Tax on dividends has been increased.

We will provide an overview of the tax benefits and drawbacks of using a company to invest in property but for a more complete discussion of all the issues we would recommend reading the Taxcafe.co.uk guide *'Using a Property Company to Save Tax'*.

Interest Relief in Companies

The restriction to residential landlords' interest relief specifically does not apply to companies (unless the company is acting in a fiduciary or representative capacity as a nominee, etc).

However, in the March 2016 Budget a new restriction on the amount of interest relief that companies can claim was announced. It is aimed principally at multinational groups that use interest payments to shift profits out of the UK but theoretically applies to all companies.

From 1st April 2017 interest relief will generally be capped at 30% of taxable earnings before interest, tax, depreciation and amortisation (EBITDA) in the UK. But most small company owners will be unaffected because the restriction will generally only apply to companies whose annual interest costs exceed £2 million.

Even for those with annual interest costs in excess of £2 million, there is an alternative option to claim interest relief on an amount equal to the average proportion of net interest to EBITDA for the worldwide group. Hence, UK companies with no associated companies overseas will also be unaffected.

Thus the new rules will not affect the vast majority of privately owned companies. However, that is not to say that the Government could not, at some point in the future, introduce other restrictions specifically targeted at privately owned property companies investing in residential property. Here we would classify the risk as 'medium'. Readers must bear these risks in mind but, for the remainder of this chapter, we will assume that the current regime for interest relief in companies continues to apply.

Tax on Rental Income

Companies that own rental property currently pay just 19% Corporation Tax on all their rental profits whereas individual landlords who are higher-rate taxpayers pay 40% Income Tax (Corporation Tax was reduced from 20% to 19% on 1st April 2017).

Individual landlords may also suffer other "penalties" including the High Income Child Benefit Charge (income over £50,000), withdrawal of their personal allowance (income over £100,000) and the 45% additional rate of tax (income over £150,000).

Property investors with large taxable rental profits may therefore end up with significantly more *after-tax* income if the properties are held inside a company. This extra income can then be reinvested to grow the business.

The gap between the tax paid by individual landlords and companies may widen even more in the years ahead, not just because individual landlords will have their interest relief restricted further, but also because the Corporation Tax rate is expected to fall to 17% in April 2020.

Example

Benny works full-time and also owns a fairly large residential property business. In 2020/21 he earns a salary of £50,000 and his property business has net rental income of £125,000 after deducting all costs except mortgage interest which comes to £40,000 per year. So his true rental profit is £85,000.

If Benny owns the properties <u>personally</u> (i.e. outside a company) he'll have a taxable rental profit of £125,000 and none of his interest will be tax deductible. His total taxable income will be £175,000.

With this much income he will lose his Income Tax personal allowance and will pay Income Tax at 20% on the first £37,500 (the assumed basic-rate band in 2020/21), 40% on the next £112,500 and 45% on the final £25,000. This will result in a tax liability of £63,750.

He will also be entitled to a tax reduction equal to 20% of his finance costs – £8,000 – so his final Income Tax bill will come to £55,750.

If instead the properties were held inside a <u>company</u> all the interest would be tax deductible and the taxable rental profit would be £85,000. Corporation tax at 17% would come to £14,450.

Benny would also pay Income Tax on his salary. The first £12,500 would be tax free (the assumed personal allowance in 2020/21) and the remaining £37,500 would be taxed at 20%, producing a total Income Tax bill of £7,500.

In summary, Benny's total annual tax bill will be £33,800 lower if he uses a company to hold his properties. This money can be rolled up inside the company and used to invest in additional properties.

Profit Extraction = Additional Tax

Clearly if Benny reinvests all of his rental profits he will be significantly better off using a company, at least when it comes to saving *Income Tax* (we'll look at Capital Gains Tax later).

But what if he needs to extract some or all of the money, for example to pay his household bills? In that case an additional Income Tax charge will typically arise.

For the average company owner, a dividend is the most tax efficient way to take money out of the company on an ongoing basis, although a small salary is often the first port of call.

This is because a salary will generally provide a Corporation Tax saving for the company itself (because it's usually a tax deductible expense). Keeping the salary small (generally no greater than the National Insurance threshold) will mean that the additional tax suffered on the salary (as opposed to a dividend) is outweighed by the Corporation Tax saving. Where the company owner has little or no other income, a small salary may even be tax free. For full details of the most tax efficient way to extract profits from a property company, see the Taxcafe.co.uk guide *'Using a Property Company to Save Tax'*.

Dividends, on the other hand, are paid out of a company's *after-tax profits*, i.e. after Corporation Tax has already been paid. However, once a small salary has been taken, dividends are generally most tax efficient.

Since 6th April 2016, new tax rates apply to dividend income (see the Taxcafe.co.uk guide *'Salary versus Dividends'*).

Dividend tax credits have been abolished, so it is no longer necessary to gross up your dividends to calculate your tax. All tax calculations will work with the amount of dividend actually paid.

The bad news is that the new tax rates for dividends are 7.5% higher than the old rates. The first £5,000 of dividend income is, however, tax free thanks to the "dividend allowance", although this will probably be cut to £2,000 from 6th April 2018.

For those receiving dividends in excess of the dividend allowance, the following Income Tax rates apply (the previous effective rates on cash dividends are included for comparison):

	Old rates	**Current rates**
Basic-rate taxpayers	0%	7.5%
Higher-rate taxpayers	25%	32.5%
Additional-rate taxpayers	30.6%	38.1%

Example continued

If Benny uses a company it will pay £14,450 Corporation Tax on its £85,000 rental profit, leaving a £70,550 after-tax profit. Let's say Benny extracts the whole £70,550 as a dividend. Added to his £50,000 salary this gives him total taxable income of £120,550.

With this much income his personal allowance will be reduced from £12,500 to £2,225 so only this much of his salary income will be tax free. The next £37,500 of his salary will be taxed at 20% and the final £10,275 will be taxed at 40%.

Turning to his dividend income, the first £2,000 will be tax free thanks to the dividend allowance and the remaining £68,550 will be taxed at 32.5%.

Benny's total Income Tax bill will be £33,889 which means he'll be left with an after-tax income of £86,661:

£50,000 salary + £70,550 dividend - £33,889 tax = £86,661

How does this compare with owning the properties personally? As we know from the previous example, Benny would face an Income Tax bill of £55,750 which means he would be left with an after-tax income of £79,250:

£50,000 salary + £85,000 rental profit - £55,750 tax = £79,250

Benny is still better off to the tune of £7,411 by using a company.

(We have ignored the National Insurance on Benny's salary throughout this example for the sake of illustration. This has no effect on his final overall saving as his National Insurance cost remains the same under both scenarios.)

Note that, for the reasons explained above, taking a small salary equal to the National Insurance threshold would have left Benny even better off. For detailed calculations of the impact of a small salary on a company owner's overall tax savings, see the Taxcafe.co.uk guide 'Using a Property Company to Save Tax'.

Not all personal versus company calculations will produce such a favourable outcome for the company investor so it is essential to do your own number crunching to determine the potential Income Tax savings.

Nevertheless it is worth mentioning that one of the advantages of being a company owner is that you have complete control over how much income you withdraw each year. This gives you significant control over your personal Income Tax bill.

Property investors who own their properties personally must pay Income Tax each year on ALL the profits of the business. By contrast, company owners only pay Income Tax on the money they actually withdraw from the company.

This often allows them to stay below key Income Tax thresholds that could result in a higher Income Tax bill.

For instance, Benny in the above example could have taken a dividend of just £50,000 instead of £70,550. This would have kept his taxable income at £100,000, allowing him to hold onto all of his Income Tax personal allowance.

Tax on Capital Gains

If you sell a rental property that you own *personally* you will, of course, be subject to Capital Gains Tax. For residential property sales, the taxable gain will typically be taxed at 28% if you are a higher-rate taxpayer (18% to the extent your basic-rate band is not used up by your income).

These rates were reduced to 20% and 10% respectively for sales of most other assets, including non-residential property, from 6th April 2016 onwards: but the old, higher, rates remain in force for residential property.

Very few property investors qualify for entrepreneurs relief, which allows up to £10m of capital gains to be taxed at just 10% (typically this relief is reserved for business owners who sell their trading business, although it can sometimes also apply to furnished holiday lets).

Companies that sell rental properties pay Corporation Tax on their capital gains and by the time we get to April 2020 the tax rate will be just 17%. Thus the tax rate faced by companies will be a lot lower than the tax rate paid by individual investors who are higher-rate taxpayers and are selling residential property.

Individuals and companies also qualify for different capital gains reliefs. Companies enjoy indexation relief which means they do not have to pay tax on any rise in the value of the property which is simply caused by inflation, as measured by the retail prices index.

Individuals, on the other hand, receive a Capital Gains Tax annual exemption which currently exempts the first £11,300 of their gains from tax (£22,600 if the property is owned by a couple).

Which relief is better varies from case to case but indexation relief is generally more valuable the more expensive the property and the longer it is held.

For example, if a property purchased by a company for £250,000 is sold 10 years later, and the retail prices index has risen by 20% over this period, the company's taxable gain will be reduced by £50,000 (£250,000 x 20%).

It's also important to point out that companies cannot benefit from the principal private residence exemption and private letting relief which can significantly reduce the Capital Gains Tax payable by individual investors who have used a property as their main residence at some point.

In summary, companies will generally pay less tax on capital gains that arise on regular residential rental properties than higher-rate taxpayer individuals will. This is beneficial when properties are being sold occasionally with the proceeds reinvested in new ones.

However, the comparison between personal and company ownership becomes much more complex when the investor wants to wind up the property business and extract money from the company.

Extracting Capital Gains from a Company

Company investors who want to sell up essentially have three main choices:

- Sell the company (i.e. sell the shares)
- Company sells the properties and pays dividends
- Company sells the properties and is wound up

Note that any loans you have made to the company can always be repaid to you tax free and it generally makes sense to withdraw these funds first before proceeding with any other steps.

Selling the Company

A company owner who sells their shares (rather than getting the company to sell the underlying properties) is subject to Capital Gains Tax at the new reduced rates. In other words, you will pay 20% tax if you are a higher-rate taxpayer, reduced to 10% to the extent that your income does not use up your basic-rate band. You will also be entitled to the annual Capital Gains Tax exemption.

Thus if a company owner sells their shares they could end up paying less Capital Gains Tax than an individual investor who owns an identical property portfolio and has to pay up to 28% tax (although the company investor would hopefully have a bigger portfolio if they've been reinvesting their less heavily taxed rental profits).

In practice, however, it may be more difficult to sell the company than the properties themselves.

Many potential buyers will shy away from buying a company because they fear that doing so may expose them to all of the company's liabilities, some of which may not be known when the company is acquired.

Furthermore, a sensible purchaser would expect to discount the value of the company's shares to take account of the Corporation Tax which would be payable on the capital gains arising within the company if it were to sell the properties which it holds.

Selling the Properties and Paying Dividends

An alternative would be to get the company to sell the properties and pay out the after-tax profits as dividends.

Paying dividends will result in double tax. The company will pay Corporation Tax on the capital gains and the company owner will pay Income Tax on the after-tax profits paid out as dividends.

By the time we get to 2020/21 this could result in a total of around £44 tax being paid on every £100 of taxable capital gain, i.e. an effective overall tax rate of almost 44%:

£100 x 17% Corporation Tax + £83 x 32.5% Income Tax = £43.975

This calculation ignores the dividend allowance which will exempt the first £2,000 of dividend income you receive from tax.

It also assumes the company owner is a higher-rate taxpayer and is subject to 32.5% Income Tax on all dividend payments from the company.

If the dividends take the company owner's income over the £100,000 threshold they will also start to lose their Income Tax personal allowance and if the dividends take the owner's income over £150,000 they will pay 38.1% tax on some of their dividend income.

It may be possible to spread the dividend payments over several tax years to avoid these two "tax penalties".

Although 44% is a lot higher than the 28% maximum Capital Gains Tax rate paid by individual investors, it is important to remember that indexation relief may result in a company having a significantly lower *taxable* capital gain on each property.

Furthermore, as we saw earlier, it is possible that a company will have enjoyed significantly higher after-tax rental profits because it will have paid Corporation Tax on its rental income instead of Income Tax. If those profits have been reinvested to build a significantly bigger property portfolio, it is possible this could more than compensate for the higher tax rate at the end.

Company owners may also be able to pay just 7.5% Income Tax if they are basic-rate taxpayers when they withdraw dividends.

By 2020/21 this could result in a total of around £23 tax being paid on every £100 of taxable capital gain, i.e. an effective overall tax rate of around 23%:

£100 x 17% Corporation Tax + £83 x 7.5% = £23.225

Extracting dividends as a basic-rate taxpayer may be possible if the dividends are only paid out when the company owner has very little income from other sources (e.g. after retiring) and can spread the dividend payments over several tax years (to utilise several years' worth of basic-rate band).

The process could also be speeded up if the company is owned by a couple so that two basic-rate bands can be used each year.

Of course property investors who own residential properties personally can adopt a similar tactic to reduce their Capital Gains Tax rate from 28% to 18%. They can spread their property sales over several years so that multiple basic-rate bands and Capital Gains Tax annual exemptions can be utilised.

So again, the benefit of using a company will probably boil down to whether the investor has been able to use the low Corporation Tax rate to build a much bigger portfolio inside a company.

Selling the Properties and Winding Up the Company

Under this scenario the company sells the properties and pays out the after-tax profits as a *capital distribution*.

A capital distribution will also result in a double tax charge. The company will pay Corporation Tax and the company owner will pay Capital Gains Tax on the after-tax profits paid out.

Winding up a company can be a very expensive process in terms of fees, especially if the company still has assets and liabilities, or has recently been in active business.

Furthermore, new rules applying from 6th April 2016 onwards mean that, in some cases, the profits distributed on a winding up may have to be treated as dividends.

These new rules apply where:

i)   The company is a 'close company',

ii)   The company owner receiving the distribution continues to carry on a similar activity to the company being wound up, and

iii)   One of the main purposes of the winding up is to achieve a reduction in Income Tax, OR
        The winding up forms part of arrangements, one of the main purposes of which is to achieve a reduction in Income Tax

At present, based on the view taken by some expert commentators, it seems likely that these new rules could apply when many property companies are wound up. This is because:

i)   The vast majority of private companies are close companies (at least 11 unconnected shareholders are needed in order to avoid this).

ii)   The owner of a property investment company would meet the second test above if they, any other company they own, their spouse, or any other close relative, continues to invest in property after the winding up.

iii)   Some expert commentators believe that HM Revenue and Customs will interpret the third test very broadly: in particular, they fear that declining to pay surplus funds out as dividends prior to the winding up could, in itself, be enough to be regarded as an 'arrangement' to reduce Income Tax.

We are not entirely convinced that the third test should be interpreted quite so broadly.

Furthermore, it is not for HM Revenue and Customs to decide the matter: that power, as in all tax disputes, ultimately lies with the courts.

Nevertheless, even if one takes a more optimistic stance on the third test, the new rules still cast a significant doubt over the treatment of profits distributed on a winding up.

Hence, unless you can make sure your company is owned by at least 11 unconnected people, or can ensure that neither you nor any of your close relatives will invest in property (directly, through a company, or through some other type of entity) after you wind up your company, it seems wisest at this point to assume that the profits distributed to you will have to be treated as a dividend.

That being so, it may make sense to pay actual dividends over the course of a few tax years (as explained above) rather than making a single large distribution when you wind up the company.

One single large distribution may lead to a loss of your personal allowance (with an expected additional tax cost of between £4,063 and £5,625 by 2020/21) plus additional rate tax on some of the funds distributed (where these take your total taxable income for the year over £150,000).

Where additional rate tax applies, this would result in a total of around £49 tax being paid on every £100 of taxable capital gain by 2020/21; i.e. an effective overall tax rate of around 49%:

$$£100 \times 17\% \text{ Corporation Tax} + £83 \times 38.1\% = £48.62$$

Remember, that adopting a phased approach to the withdrawal of profits from your company should enable you to enjoy the overall effective rates of around 44% or even 23% described above.

A More Optimistic View

At this stage, we would advocate planning on the basis that the new rules regarding profits distributed on a winding up will apply when you come to sell your portfolio. Hence the previous strategy of paying sale proceeds out as dividends will be preferable and you should plan accordingly.

However, it may be that by the time you do come to sell your portfolio, the third test might have been examined in court and may not be interpreted quite so widely as some people are currently suggesting. Or you may have managed to ensure that you do not meet one of the first two tests (all three tests must be met for you to be caught by the new rules).

Either way, you may by then be in a position to wind up your company without having the profits distributed on the winding up taxed as a dividend.

If that is the case then you would be able to get your hands on all the money in a single tax year without being subject to the extortionate Income Tax rates that apply when large dividend payments are received.

As with dividends, however, this approach will still result in a double tax charge. When the company sells the properties it will pay Corporation Tax on its capital gains and you will pay Capital Gains Tax on the proceeds distributed.

Remember, as explained above, any loans you have made to the company should generally be repaid to you first and these sums will be tax free.

When calculating your Capital Gains Tax, you can also deduct the amount you originally invested in the company as share capital. We generally advise investors to keep their company's share capital to a small nominal sum, such as £100, and to make any further investments in the company by way of loan. Loans can easily be repaid whenever the company has the funds to do so. For this reason, they are generally preferable.

Share capital can only be repaid under certain limited circumstances. This includes a winding up, although this point is currently under review, so we may see some restrictions in future. This reinforces the point that loans are generally preferable: with just a small nominal sum being invested as share capital.

Either way, the amount which you originally invested will not be subject to Capital Gains Tax. For example, if the company is left with £250,000 after selling the properties and paying Corporation Tax, the company owner will receive a total of £250,000. If they originally invested, say, £100,000 in the company, their taxable capital gain will be £150,000. (Technically, if the original investment was a loan, the company owner is receiving a loan repayment of £100,000 and a taxable capital distribution of £150,000.)

By the time we get to 2020/21 the double tax charge could result in a total of around £34 tax being paid on every £100 of taxable capital gain, i.e. an effective overall tax rate of around 34%:

£100 x 17% Corporation Tax + £83 x 20% Capital Gains Tax = £33.60

Some of the gain may be taxed at just 10% if your basic-rate band has not been used up by your income and the Capital Gains Tax annual exemption will also reduce the overall tax bill by a few thousand pounds.

As usual, any overall benefit that is to be enjoyed by using a company will probably boil down to whether the investor has been able to use the low Corporation Tax rate to build a much bigger portfolio inside a company.

The Effective Corporation Tax Rate

It is important to remember that the effective rate of Corporation Tax paid by the company will generally be reduced thanks to indexation relief. If we assume an effective Corporation Tax rate of just 8.5% (i.e. half of the gains in the company being exempted by indexation relief), we see between around £15 and £43 of tax being paid on every £100 of capital gain arising, i.e. effective overall tax rates of between around 15% and 43%:

Dividends taxed at basic rate:

£100 x 8.5% Corporation Tax + £91.50 x 7.5% Income Tax = £15.36

Dividends taxed at higher rate:

£100 x 8.5% Corporation Tax + £91.50 x 32.5% Income Tax = £38.24

Dividends taxed at additional rate:

£100 x 8.5% Corporation Tax + £91.50 x 38.1% Income Tax = £43.36

Distributions taxed as capital gains:

£100 x 8.5% Corporation Tax + £91.50 x 20% CGT = £26.80

A rate of 15% appears highly beneficial but it must be remembered that this can only be achieved by a basic-rate taxpayer.

The potential rate of 26.8% is only marginally better than the 28% Capital Gains Tax that would be paid if the properties were held personally and, as discussed above, there are doubts over whether this can be achieved in some cases.

The reality in many cases, therefore, is that the overall rate could remain significantly higher than the Capital Gains Tax payable by an individual investor.

Nevertheless, what we must always remember is that throughout the intervening years there will have been considerable tax savings on any rental income or sale proceeds reinvested within the company and the property portfolio may ultimately be considerably larger as a result.

Even when profits have been paid out as dividends in previous years, the cumulative tax savings which the company owner has enjoyed may still outweigh the extra tax arising when the portfolio is eventually sold. Look at Benny in our example above: he saved £7,411 a year even when he took all of his company's after tax profits as dividends!

So, does the company pay off in the end? That's a question that every property investor has to look at for themselves, based on their own circumstances, their long-term goals, and their own view of future changes to property values, rental yields, interest rates, inflation and the UK tax regime.

Future Tax Changes

It's important to make one crucial final point:

Any tax benefit you hope to obtain by using a company could be taken away at the stroke of a pen.

Just as George Osborne practically napalmed landlords before running off to his high paid job in the City, any future Chancellor could drop a similar tax bombshell on property company owners.

Company owners have experienced numerous ups and downs going back to the days when Gordon Brown was Chancellor and beyond. The most recent announcement is an expected cut in the tax-free allowance for dividends from £5,000 to £2,000 in April 2018. This will result in some higher-rate taxpayers paying an additional £975 tax every year.

Throughout 2016 the Orwellian sounding "Office of Tax Simplification" (OTS) investigated a system of "look through" taxation for certain small companies.

A look through system, if made compulsory, would take away the tax benefits of using a company. Under look through taxation, instead of paying Corporation Tax, certain company owners would pay Income Tax and National Insurance on all the profits of the business, just like sole traders and partnerships do.

One of the advantages of using a company is that you can smooth your income and control your Income Tax bill by paying yourself dividends as and when you like. Those who wish to grow their businesses can retain profits inside the company, in which case the only tax payable is 19% Corporation Tax (falling to 17% in 2020).

Fortunately, the OTS has decided not to recommend look through taxation because it would not simplify the tax system and would harm investment. So, hopefully, at least for now, this specific threat has gone away.

Nevertheless the Government seems determined to narrow the gap between the tax paid by regular employees, the self-employed and company owners. Thus we cannot rule out further tax increases at some point in the future.

Chapter 24

Getting Existing Property into a Company

Introduction

Using a company is certainly possible when it comes to making new property acquisitions. The biggest challenge is getting *existing* properties that you already own into a company.

The basic problem with transferring anything into your company is the fact that you and the company are 'connected'. Any transfers of assets between you and the company will be deemed to take place at market value for Capital Gains Tax purposes.

Potentially, therefore, you could face a huge tax bill if you try to transfer existing properties into a company.

Furthermore, any transfer of property to a connected company will also be deemed to take place at market value for Stamp Duty Land Tax purposes. Companies acquiring residential property will be subject to the higher Stamp Duty Land Tax rates detailed in Chapter 22. These higher rates apply to every residential property in England, Wales or Northern Ireland which is acquired by a company; including both purchases and transfers from the company's owner (see Chapter 22 regarding property in Wales).

Multiple dwellings relief can be claimed on any simultaneous transfer of two or more residential dwellings. For a simultaneous transfer of six or more dwellings, the company can also elect to use the non-residential Stamp Duty Land Tax rates.

Non-residential Stamp Duty Land Tax rates were changed in the 2016 Budget and a new system of progressive rates (or a 'slice' system) applies from 17th March 2016 onwards:

- First £150,000:   0%
- £150,000 - £250,000:   2%
- Over £250,000:   5%

Example

*Michelle has eight residential rental properties worth a total of £1.2m.
She transfers them to her own company.*

*Under basic principles, the company would have to pay Stamp Duty
Land Tax at the higher residential rates as follows:*

£125,000 x 3% = £3,750
£125,000 x 5% = £6,250
£675,000 x 8% = £54,000
£275,000 x 13% = £35,750
Total: £99,750

*Using multiple dwellings relief, however, the Stamp Duty Land Tax
would be based on the average value of each property: £150,000; as
follows:*

£125,000 x 3% = £3,750
£25,000 x 5%   = £1,250
Total per property: £5,000
Total for eight properties: £40,000 (£5,000 x 8)

*Alternatively, the company could elect to pay Stamp Duty Land Tax at
non-residential rates, as follows:*

£150,000 x 0% = £0
£100,000 x 2% = £2,000
£950,000 x 5% = £47,500
Total: £49,500

Multiple dwellings relief is the best option in Michelle's case, but
the non-residential rates will sometimes produce a better result in
other cases (where available).

It is important to remember that multiple dwellings relief is based
on the number of 'dwellings', not the number of properties.

Hence, for example, if one of Michelle's properties were divided
into three self-contained flats, there would be ten dwellings in
total and the average value of each 'dwelling' would be just
£120,000. The Stamp Duty Land Tax payable on the transfer, with
multiple dwellings relief, would then reduce to £36,000:

£120,000 x 3% = £3,600 x 10 = £36,000

Property in Scotland

Properties located in Scotland are subject to Land and Buildings Transaction Tax rather than Stamp Duty Land Tax. However, transfers of property to a connected company are again deemed to take place at market value for Land and Buildings Transaction Tax purposes. The 3% surcharge again applies to every residential property in Scotland acquired by a company, either by way of purchase or by way of a transfer from the company's owner.

As explained in Chapter 22, multiple dwellings relief operates in a different way in Scotland: it is generally based on the value of each individual dwelling within the transaction. Note, once again, however, that the relief is based on the value of each 'dwelling' rather than each property.

Multiple dwellings relief cannot reduce the total Land and Buildings Transaction Tax charge to less than 25% of what it would have been without the relief.

A simultaneous transfer of six or more dwellings located in Scotland may again alternatively be taxed at the non-residential rates of Land and Buildings Transaction Tax, which are:

- First £150,000:   0%
- £150,000 - £350,000:   3%
- Over £350,000:   4.5%

Example
Paul transfers five Scottish residential properties to his own company. One of them is a croft in Assynt worth £30,000, two are houses in Edinburgh worth £275,000 each and the other two are flats in Falkirk worth £90,000 each. Without multiple dwellings relief, the Land and Buildings Transaction Tax payable on the total value of £760,000 would be:

£145,000 x 3% = £4,350
£105,000 x 5% = £5,250
£75,000   x 8% = £6,000
£425,000 x 13% = £55,250
£10,000   x 15% = £1,500
Total: £72,350

Using multiple dwellings relief, however, the Land and Buildings Transaction Tax would be based on the individual value of each property, as follows:

Croft: £30,000 x 0% = £0 x 1 = £0

Falkirk flats: £90,000 x 3% = £2,700 x 2 = £5,400

Edinburgh houses:
£145,000 x 3% = £4,350
£105,000 x 5% = £5,250
£25,000   x 8% = £2,000
Total: £11,600 x 2 = £23,200

Total for all properties: £28,600

This exceeds 25% of the charge without multiple dwellings relief, so this is the charge that will apply.

Example Revisited

Let us now suppose that one of Paul's Edinburgh houses has been divided into two self-contained flats. This means that he is now transferring six dwellings and the company may elect to use the non-residential Land and Buildings Transaction Tax rates based on the total value of the properties transferred (£760,000):

£150,000 x 0%   = £0
£200,000 x 3%   = £6,000
£410,000 x 4.5% = £18,450
Total: £24,450

The charge under multiple dwellings relief would also now be different, as the charge on the two Edinburgh flats (taken together) would now be £8,250 (£275,000 x 3%) instead of £11,600, reducing the overall charge by £3,350, from £28,600 to £25,250.

Nonetheless, the option to use non-residential rates remains preferable.

Hence, once again, the fact that the charge is based on the number of 'dwellings' rather than the number of properties has led to a tax saving. Paul would even have saved tax if he had used an additional property worth anything up to £92,000 in order to increase the number of dwellings transferred: although probably not if he had to buy it first.

Partnerships

It may be possible to transfer properties which are part of a property business run by a partnership into a company and enjoy substantial or complete exemption from either Stamp Duty Land Tax or Land and Buildings Transaction Tax (as appropriate).

To obtain the exemption, the company needs to be 'connected' with one or more of the partners. If it is 'connected' with all/both of the partners, complete exemption is possible. The good news is that a company will generally be 'connected' with all/both of the partners if all/both of those partners are:

- Spouses or civil partners,
- Siblings, or
- Parents and their adult children

And these individuals also own the company.

Hence, the most obvious example is where a married couple, or a family, have been running a property business as a partnership and they transfer the business to their own company. In many such cases, complete exemption from Stamp Duty Land Tax or Land and Buildings Transaction Tax will be possible.

The exemption applies equally to limited liability partnerships (although these are not usually a good medium through which to invest in property due to some even more restrictive rules on interest relief).

Some people have suggested that a property portfolio which is jointly owned by a married couple, or by any two individuals, is effectively a partnership, even if it has not been formally constituted as one. Unfortunately, this is not the case, and a formally constituted partnership, which has submitted partnership tax returns, is needed for the exemption to apply.

Others are suggesting that it is only necessary to form a partnership for a brief period before transferring property into a company in order to obtain the exemption. We are not comfortable with this idea as we feel that some of the applicable anti-avoidance legislation could be used to overturn the exemption in such a case.

One thing which is clear, however, is that a transfer of property from a long-term, well established, property partnership run by a married couple, or other qualifying relatives, to a company owned by the same individuals is completely exempt from both Stamp Duty Land Tax and Land and Buildings Transaction Tax.

However, the rules governing this exemption are highly complex, so professional advice is essential.

Incorporation Relief

As discussed above, the transfer of property into a company could potentially result in significant tax costs.

As far as Capital Gains Tax is concerned, there is an important relief available which may potentially resolve the problem in some cases: incorporation relief.

If a successful claim for incorporation relief is made the property investor will achieve a tax-free uplift in the base cost of all of their properties to current market value.

As residential investment properties would be subject to Capital Gains Tax at 18% or 28% in the transferor's own hands, the uplift in base costs could provide the potential to make massive savings.

Once in the company, properties could generally eventually be sold with a Corporation Tax exposure of just 17% of the future increase in their value above the rate of retail price inflation.

Incorporation relief should be available whenever any 'business' is transferred to a company wholly or partly in exchange for shares. The problem is that there is no statutory definition of what constitutes a business for the purposes of incorporation relief.

Until recently, there was no relevant case law to fall back on either, but the recent case of 'Elisabeth Moyne Ramsay v Revenue and Customs Commissioners' (the 'Ramsay case') has finally shed some light on this issue.

It is important to understand that this decision does not necessarily mean that all property investment businesses will qualify for incorporation relief; it only gives us an indication of which businesses might qualify.

Furthermore, whilst it was decided that Mrs Ramsay did indeed have a qualifying business, the case does not even draw an accurate 'borderline' which the rest of us can use to decide whether a qualifying business exists in other cases. This is because the judge made it very clear that he accepted that Mrs Ramsay had a qualifying business based on all the facts 'taken overall' rather than because of any single factor alone.

Hence, in other cases, where only some of the same factors are present as in the Ramsay case, it will still be unclear as to whether a qualifying business exists for the purposes of incorporation relief.

Nonetheless, it is worth listing some of the factors which may have acted in Mrs Ramsay's favour:

- Her property business consisted of a joint interest in a single property divided into 10 self-contained flats

- The property had extensive communal areas, as well as a garden, a car park and some garages

- Substantial repairs and maintenance work was carried out on the communal areas, garden, car park and garages

- Mrs Ramsay carried out some of this work personally

- Additional assistance was provided to one elderly tenant

- Prior to the transfer of the property to a company, Mr and Mrs Ramsay carried out some preparatory work regarding a proposed project to refurbish and redevelop the property

- Mrs Ramsay and her husband spent approximately 20 hours per week on activities related to the property

- Neither of them had any other occupation during the relevant period

Based on these facts, the judge concluded:

"that the activity undertaken in respect of the property, again taken overall, was sufficient in nature and extent to amount to a business for the purpose of [incorporation relief]. Although each of the activities could equally well have been undertaken by someone who was a mere property investor, where the degree of activity outweighs what might normally be expected to be carried out by a mere passive investor, even a diligent and conscientious one, that will in my judgment amount to a business."

So, Mrs Ramsay qualified but the judge also made the point that another owner of investment property might only be a 'passive investor' who would not qualify and there was no single factor which determined this distinction: it was down to the degree of activity undertaken by the investor.

Where Does The Ramsay Case Leave Us?

The Ramsay case has certainly improved the chances of some property investors qualifying for incorporation relief.

Those who can demonstrate that their business activities are equal in scope to Mrs Ramsay's (or greater) should now be able to claim incorporation relief.

Nonetheless, despite the helpful result in the Ramsay case, the question of whether incorporation relief might be available for the vast majority of other property investment businesses still remains uncertain. The danger in many cases is that the business could be regarded as a 'passive investment'. HM Revenue and Customs takes the stance that the mere holding of investment property and collection of rent does not constitute a business for incorporation relief purposes.

One of the major problems is that to get the relief, one must transfer the entire business to the company. If relief is not then forthcoming, there could be a substantial Capital Gains Tax bill.

Furthermore, whether relief is obtained or not, Stamp Duty Land Tax or Land and Buildings Transaction Tax will usually be payable on the market value of the properties transferred (subject to the partnership exemption and other available reliefs discussed above).

So, the stakes are high and the outcome will often be uncertain!

Before even considering whether to attempt an incorporation relief claim, it would be necessary to take a very detailed look at the particular circumstances of the property business in question and establish whether it amounts to more than 'the mere passive holding of investments'.

The Ramsay case will be helpful in carrying out this exercise, but it will be pretty rare for the property owner's circumstances to be exactly the same as Mrs Ramsay's!

So, the question remains: just how much more than passive investment does the business need to be in order to qualify? As much as Mrs Ramsay, or more, is enough: we know that now. But how much less than Mrs Ramsay might suffice: we still do not know!

Some of the key points which need to be considered after the Ramsay case are whether it is necessary for:

- The property to contain substantial communal areas
- The owner to carry out repairs and maintenance personally
- The property business to be the owner's only occupation
- The owner to be actively looking at ways to improve the capital value or rental yield of their property

Mrs Ramsay satisfied all of these points. The position where only some of these points are satisfied remains uncertain.

Some people are now arguing that it is only necessary to satisfy the third point: that the business is the owner's only occupation. This is highly persuasive, but we do not agree that this can be seen as the single determining factor.

As always, we have to come back to the judge's comments in the case: is the activity undertaken, taken overall, sufficient to amount to a business? You might think so, but will the judge?

Nonetheless, despite these doubts, there is room for a degree of optimism and many more substantial property businesses should now qualify for incorporation relief: but professional advice is essential!

Chapter 25

Using a Company: Mortgage Issues

Mortgages are available to company owners but the choice is fairly limited and the interest rates and arrangement fees may be higher.

In other words, some of what you gain from having full tax relief on your interest payments could be lost by paying a higher interest rate!

We asked Ray Boulger, senior technical manager at mortgage broker John Charcol, to comment on the market for company mortgages and are grateful for the following overview:

The number of lenders offering a mortgage on a property owned by a company has increased significantly over the last year. This is because the income tax changes on Buy to Let properties owned in a personal name has resulted in an increased proportion of purchases being in a company name, making this sector more attractive to lenders in view of the increased demand.

As a result of increased competition many lenders who offer BTL mortgages to a company no longer charge a higher interest rate than for a mortgage in a personal name, although some arrangement fees are higher. However, because the majority of lenders still do not offer a mortgage to a company it is likely that the most competitive interest rates will not be available for purchases in a company name.

Lenders generally insist on using a separate special purpose vehicle (SPV), i.e. a company used solely for buy-to-let property and not to conduct other business activities. Some lenders are happy for an SPV to own more than one property, whereas others prefer just one property per SPV.

As far as existing properties are concerned, a personal borrower considering putting the property into a company would have to redeem any existing mortgage and apply for a new mortgage in the company's name. If their existing mortgage happened to be with one of the few lenders that offer mortgages to limited companies it is probable the lender will help facilitate a smooth transfer to keep the business but a new application would have to be made and the interest rate may be different. A new arrangement fee would also be charged. Lenders sometimes insist on personal guarantees.

Because tax is charged on the profit when a BTL property is held by a company, compared to the whole rental income being added to taxable income when held in a personal name, some lenders reflect this lower tax liability by applying a lower ratio requirement for interest cover, typically 125% instead of 145%. The effect of this is that it is sometimes possible to borrow more if a property is in a company name.

For large amounts, whether a single property or a portfolio, private banks will generally be happy to lend to SPVs, possibly at similar rates to personal customers. The commercial arms of some banks will also lend to SPVs, but normally charge more than their mortgage division would for a standard buy-to-let mortgage.

Portfolio Landlords

From 1st October 2017 the PRA has instructed lenders to apply "specialist underwriting" to applications from landlords with four or more mortgaged properties, whereas at present most lenders just check affordability for the property being mortgaged.

It is still unclear exactly what this specialist approach will entail, and there is scope for different lenders to interpret the rules differently, but it is certainly going to require a more detailed review of a landlord's business model and their ability to manage risk.

Lenders may want to stress test a landlord's entire portfolio against their interest cover ratio (ICR) as well as stress testing interest rates, which they are already required to do unless the initial interest rate is fixed for at least 5 years.

They may request rental income accounts and possibly a business plan to support an application, all of which will undoubtedly lead to longer offer times as underwriters will need to spend more time assessing applications and it could result in reduced loan sizes being agreed if stress testing is not met across the portfolio.

In the short term, these new processes are likely to mean that competition will diminish as lenders spend time and money to train staff and update systems to cope with the changes, with some deciding that the cost outweighs the benefit and choosing to exit this sector entirely. The knock-on effect for the lenders that are ready to operate in this market on 1st October is likely to be an increase in applications, which in turn will lead to a bottle neck and further offer delays.

Thus, the process of obtaining a new mortgage, including a remortgage, for portfolio landlords is going to take longer after September, so those landlords that have obtained tax advice and want to continue expanding their portfolio need to bear this in mind. There may be some options to release funds for expansion without having a specific property in mind as yet.

Deeds of Trust/Beneficial Interest Trusts

In some cases, it may be possible to transfer the beneficial interest in properties to a company without disturbing the existing mortgage arrangements by using a Deed of Trust (also known as a Beneficial Interest Trust).

This will have the same consequences for both Capital Gains Tax and Stamp Duty Land Tax or Land and Buildings Transaction Tax as a transfer of the legal title.

This is a complex arrangement and we strongly recommend taking legal advice regarding the validity of the arrangement and the consequences regarding the outstanding mortgages. Our understanding is that it would be the property owner's legal obligation to ensure that their mortgage lenders are fully advised of the arrangement. Furthermore, some lenders would not permit such an arrangement.

Chapter 26

Other Ways to Save Tax by Using a Company

In Chapters 23 and 24, we looked at the potential benefits of holding property in a company, as well as the many complexities involved in transferring property to a company.

There may, however, be other ways to save tax by using a company which do not involve the company actually owning any property.

Leasing Property to Your Own Company

You can reduce the amount of tax you pay personally by leasing property to your own company, which will then rent the property to your tenants.

This could be a useful means to avoid exposure to higher rate tax on profits which you are not actually making.

Example
It is 2020/21 and Margaret has a salary of £40,000 and a small portfolio of rental property yielding total gross rental income of £25,000. She pays mortgage interest on her rental properties totalling £10,000 and other annual costs of £5,000, giving her a true rental profit of £10,000.

Margaret's taxable rental profit will be £20,000 (£25,000 - £5,000), of which £10,000 will fall into her basic rate band and get taxed at 20% and £10,000 will be taxed at 40%. Her tax liability therefore totals £6,000.

Margaret can then claim a tax reduction of £2,000 (£10,000 x 20%) in respect of her mortgage interest, leaving her with a net tax bill of £4,000 and after tax income from her property business of £6,000.

Instead of this, however, Margaret leases her properties to her company for £10,500 per year. She still pays the same amount of mortgage interest but her annual costs fall to just £500, leaving her in a 'true' position of break even.

Her taxable rental profit will now be £10,000 (£10,500 - £500) which will all be taxed at basic rate, meaning that her tax reduction for mortgage interest will leave her with no tax to pay overall.

The company makes a rental profit of £10,000 (£25,000 rent received less lease payments of £10,500 and the remaining £4,500 of annual costs). After paying Corporation Tax at 17%, it is left with an after tax profit of £8,300.

Margaret can take up to £2,000 of the company's after tax profit as a tax-free dividend but will suffer Income Tax at 32.5% on any excess.

She will therefore be left with total after tax income between £6,252 and £8,300, depending on how much she retains within the company. However, if she extracts all of her company profits she will be just £252 better off overall.

This arrangement has some potential drawbacks. There will be significant legal and professional costs involved which will outweigh an annual saving of just £252 (but could be worthwhile on a bigger scale).

If the lease to the company is for a long enough period to have a 'net present value' in excess of £125,000 then Stamp Duty Land Tax will be payable at 1% on the excess (see the Taxcafe.co.uk guide *'How to Save Property Tax'* for further details).

The charges under the lease must not exceed a normal commercial 'arm's length' rate. However, it appears that there is no problem with them being lower.

Lastly, it may be necessary to get the mortgage lender's permission for the arrangement and this will not always be forthcoming. Legal advice is again essential.

Using a Property Management Company

In Chapter 13, we looked at the possibility of reducing the taxable profits on your property business by paying management fees to some form of connected entity. We expressed some reservations regarding this arrangement and stressed the importance for it to have an appropriate level of commercial substance.

Subject to these reservations (and the two 'words of warning' which we also emphasised), it is possible for a landlord to use a property management company to reduce their own tax burden.

Example
Carter is an additional rate taxpayer with a large property portfolio generating annual gross rents of £400,000. In 2020/21, he decides to sub-contract the management of his properties to a new property management company, Danco Property Services Limited.

Danco Property Services Limited charges Carter 15% of the gross annual rents on the properties (£60,000) as a service charge for managing the portfolio. Naturally, the company also ends up bearing some of the expenses in running the property portfolio and these amount to £6,000.

Carter's taxable income will now be reduced by £54,000 (£60,000 - £6,000), saving him £24,300 in Income Tax (at 45%). Meanwhile, Danco Property Services Limited will have annual profits of £54,000, giving it a Corporation Tax bill, at 17%, of £9,180.

The overall tax paid by Carter and Danco Property Services Limited combined is thus reduced by £15,120 (£24,300 - £9,180).

As usual, however, it doesn't work quite so well if the company's profits are extracted. If Carter takes out all of the company's after-tax profit of £44,820 as a dividend, he will pay additional Income Tax of £16,314:

£44,820 less £2,000 dividend allowance = £42,820 x 38.1% = £16,314

*This turns the £15,120 saving into an overall additional tax **cost** of £1,194!*

For Carter to be able to claim a valid Income Tax deduction for the company's management fees, he must be able to show that they were incurred wholly and exclusively for the benefit of his property rental business. In other words, there must be a genuine provision of services by the company.

Furthermore, as explained in Chapter 13, this type of arrangement is only likely to be valid where the property management company has other unconnected clients.

This, in turn, may create another problem: if the total level of management fees (and other charges, commission, or sales) charged by the company exceeds the VAT registration threshold, it will need to register for and charge VAT at 20%.

If, as will generally be the case, the individual landlord is unable to recover this VAT, it will completely undo the whole purpose of the exercise and could turn it into a costly mess!

Example continued
Danco Property Services Limited has a number of other clients and the fees charged to Carter take its total gross income over the VAT registration threshold. It therefore has to start charging VAT at 20%.

Carter now pays management fees totalling £72,000 (£60,000 + 20%), so his taxable income is reduced by £66,000 (£72,000 - £6,000) and his Income Tax bill reduces by £29,700 (£66,000 x 45%).

The company is now able to recover £1,000 of input VAT included within its annual costs of £6,000, so the net amount of VAT paid over to HM Revenue and Customs in respect of its contract with Carter is £11,000 (£60,000 x 20% = £12,000 - £1,000 = £11,000).

The company's taxable profit on its contract with Carter is now £55,000 (£1,000 more than before due to the recovery of input VAT), giving it a Corporation Tax bill, at 17%, of £9,350.

The overall net position is now as follows:
Income tax saved by Carter:	*£29,700*
Less:	
VAT paid by company:	*£11,000*
Corporation tax paid by company:	*£9,350*
Equals a net saving of:	*£9,350*

(It is a mere coincidence that the overall net saving happens to equal the Corporation Tax paid by the company in this particular case!)

*BUT, this net saving is reliant on Carter leaving after tax profits of £45,650 in the company. If he takes these out as a dividend, he will pay a further £16,631 in Income Tax and there will be an overall tax **cost** of £7,281!*

As we can see, using your own property management company carries a number of potential pitfalls and, done badly, could end up costing a great deal of extra tax.

However, subject to all of our reservations, and most especially our 'words of warning' in Chapter 13, if done well it could save a significant amount of tax.

Doing it 'well' will include reinvesting some or all of the company's after tax profits within the company and managing the company's business carefully so that, whilst it does take on other, unconnected clients, its total gross income remains below the VAT registration threshold.

Furthermore, if you manage to do it 'well', even greater tax savings may be possible if the company is owned by and/or employs your spouse, partner or other family members.

Chapter 27

The New Cash Basis for Landlords

Starting on 6th April 2017, most unincorporated property businesses (i.e. individual landlords) can use the "cash basis" to calculate their tax.

The cash basis is open to landlords with total gross annual rental income (before deducting **any** expenses) of £150,000 or less.

Those who use the cash basis only pay tax on the rental income they've actually *received* during the year. If a tenant should have paid rent but hasn't, it is not taxable. By the same token, landlords are only able to claim tax relief for expenses they've actually *paid* during the year.

By contrast, under traditional accruals accounting (also know as GAAP accounting) income is included when it is earned, even if it hasn't been received yet, and expenses are included when they are incurred, even if they haven't been paid yet. (A bad debt expense may, of course, eventually be claimed where it becomes unlikely that income which was due will ever be received.)

Note that the cash basis is now the **default** method landlords must use to calculate their tax, unless they opt out or their gross rental income for the year exceeds £150,000. If they opt out they can use accruals accounting instead.

Landlords who would otherwise fall into the cash basis must make the election to opt out every year when they complete their tax returns (for 2017/18 onwards).

Partnerships can use the new cash basis as long as all the partners are individuals. Companies, trusts, limited liability partnerships, and partnerships with one or more corporate partners are excluded.

Joint owners can decide independently whether or not to use the cash basis, unless they're a married couple or civil partners, in which case they must both use the same basis.

If spouses or civil partners each have a separate rental business but own even one rental property jointly, they will both have to use the same basis for their entire property business.

Overseas and UK property businesses are treated as separate businesses, so a separate decision can be made for each business.

If the landlord also has a separate trading business, a separate decision can be taken for the trading and property businesses.

The cost of replacement furnishings may be claimed on the same basis as other landlords using normal accounting. Landlords may not claim the initial costs of furnishing a property or the cost of additional items.

Transitional rules apply in the year that a landlord enters or leaves the cash basis. Broadly speaking, these rules are designed to ensure that all income is taxed once, but only once, and all qualifying expenses are relieved once, but only once.

Timing Issues

Generally speaking, where a landlord has the same marginal tax rate each year, it usually makes sense to defer taxable income and accelerate deductible expenditure wherever possible. Hence, the cash basis will generally be disadvantageous for landlords in the long run because, under the cash basis:

- Rent becomes fully taxable on receipt, even if it relates to a period which extends beyond the end of the tax year

- Expenses which have been incurred but not yet paid at the end of the tax year cannot be claimed

Over the next few years, however, the cash basis may prove advantageous in some cases as many landlords face increases in their marginal tax rate. Under these circumstances, accelerating taxable income or deferring deductible expenditure may lead to considerable tax savings (as we saw in Chapter 12).

Furthermore, the cash basis opens up more opportunities to defer deductible expenditure. For example, allowable repairs expenditure could be carried out during one tax year but paid for in a later year when the landlord has a higher marginal tax rate.

As discussed in Chapter 12, some expenditure is related to a specific time period and hence, under traditional accruals accounting, will generally have to be claimed as an expense of that period. Under the cash basis however, a landlord could delay paying things like ground rent and utility bills for a short period so that they may be claimed in a later year when the landlord has a higher marginal tax rate. Changing the payment of insurance premiums from a single payment to a monthly direct debit could also have a similar beneficial effect.

Naturally, it is generally only possible to delay payments for a short period and the impact on your relationship with the payees needs to be considered.

Finance Costs under the Cash Basis

Under the different cash basis for *trading* businesses, a deduction of no more than £500 is allowed for interest expenses on cash borrowings. Under the new cash basis for *property* businesses, there is a different restriction (see below) but it only applies in limited circumstances.

Thus most landlords who decide to use the cash basis will be able to claim all their finance costs (including loan arrangement fees) *as they are paid*, subject to the tax relief restriction which is the focus of this guide. (Adding arrangement fees to the loan counts as *paid* for this purpose.)

By contrast, under traditional accruals accounting, loan arrangement fees generally cannot be claimed in one go in the year they are paid and have to be spread over several years (see Chapter 14). When we get to 2020/21 these costs will only attract tax relief at 20%.

Thus landlords who use the cash basis and pay loan arrangement fees this year may be able to enjoy more tax relief than landlords who use traditional accruals accounting.

For a typical higher-rate taxpayer with a marginal tax rate of 40%, the effective rate of relief for their finance costs during the current 2017/18 tax year is 35%.

For example, if you are a higher-rate taxpayer and incur mortgage arrangement fees of £10,000 in 2017/18, you will enjoy tax relief of £3,500 under the cash basis (£10,000 x 35%). Under traditional accruals accounting, this cost would generally have to be spread over several years and some of it might therefore attract tax relief at just 20%.

The tax and accounting treatment applying to loan arrangement fees also extends to all professional and other costs associated with obtaining long-term loan finance (including mortgages). For further details see the Taxcafe.co.uk guide *'How to Save Property Tax'*.

Tax Relief Restrictions under the Cash Basis

Generally speaking, using the cash basis only alters the timing of when expenses may be claimed for tax purposes (i.e. changing it from when the expense is *incurred*, to when it is *paid*). However, there are two circumstances under which the *total* amount of expenses claimed may be restricted under the cash basis.

Firstly, there is a further restriction on interest relief where additional borrowings are taken out for business purposes and these additional borrowings take the total amount borrowed against a property beyond that property's original value when first rented out.

Secondly, it also appears that some abortive expenditure relating to potential purchases of new property which are abandoned may not be allowable under the cash basis. (Such expenses would normally be allowable under traditional accruals accounting provided that a final decision to purchase the property had not yet been made at the time the expense was incurred – see the Taxcafe.co.uk guide *'How to Save Property Tax'* for further details.)

Comparing Cash and Accruals

To summarise some of the points outlined in this chapter, let's take a look at a final example.

Example

Safiya is a higher rate taxpayer. During the 2017/18 tax year she receives rent totalling £120,000, pays interest of £70,000 and incurs other expenses of £20,000, including £1,000 for some surveys on properties she later decided not to buy and £5,000 for some roof repairs carried out in March 2018 which she pays in late April.

£4,000 of Safiya's interest expense relates to some additional borrowing she took out a couple of years ago in order to fund the cost of some urgent repairs to her properties. Although it is beyond doubt that this additional borrowing was for purely business reasons, it took her total borrowings above the total value of all of her properties when they were each rented out for the first time.

£12,000 of Safiya's income was received in the first five days of April 2018 and relates to the rent due for the whole of that month.

Safiya's accountant works out her profit under traditional accruals accounting principles as follows:

Income due for the year	*£110,000*
(£120,000 - £12,000 x 25/30)	
Less expenses:	
Interest	*£70,000*
Other expenses incurred	*£20,000*
Accrued accountancy fees	*£2,000*
Rental profit	*£18,000*

£17,500, or 25%, of Safiya's interest expense will be added back to profit for tax purposes and will instead give rise to a tax deduction at basic rate.

If Safiya does not elect to use traditional accruals accounting principles, she will fall into the cash basis by default and her profit will then be calculated as follows:

Income received in the year	*£120,000*
Less expenses paid in the year:	
Interest (£70,000 - £4,000)	*£66,000*
Other	*£14,000*
(£15,000 less survey costs not allowed £1,000)	
Net rental income	*£40,000*

£16,500, or 25%, of Safiya's allowable interest will be added to her income for tax purposes and will instead give rise to a tax deduction at basic rate.

As we can see, the cash basis would cause a considerable increase in Safiya's tax liability for 2017/18. Her taxable rental income will increase from £35,500 (£18,000 + £17,500) to £56,500 (£40,000 + £16,500), costing her an extra £8,400 in Income Tax (£21,000 x 40%). Her interest eligible for a tax reduction at basic rate will also be reduced from £17,500 to £16,500, losing her a further £200 in tax relief. Overall, her tax bill is increased by £8,600.

However, it is worth pointing out that the £21,000 increase in her taxable income is made up of a number of elements, some of which are only timing differences which will reverse in a later year, and some of which are 'absolute' – i.e. a loss of relief which will not reverse. These can be summarised as follows:

Timing differences	
Rental income accelerated	*£10,000*
Unpaid repair bill	*£5,000*
Accrued accountancy fees	*£2,000*
Total	*£17,000*
Absolute differences	
Abortive survey fees	*£1,000*
Disallowed interest	
(£4,000 x 75%)	*£3,000*
Total	*£4,000*

She has also lost out on a tax reduction for a further £1,000 of disallowed interest (£4,000 x 25%).

Let us now suppose that the timing differences will reverse the following year when Safiya's marginal tax rate is 60% (i.e. her taxable income exceeds £100,000 – see Chapter 12 for further explanation of the marginal rate arising). This will result in a tax saving for 2018/19 of £10,200 (£17,000 x 60%).

However, Safiya will again lose out on tax relief for £4,000 of her interest cost. This time this will cost her additional Income Tax totalling £1,600 (£2,000 x 60% + £2,000 x 20%).

Her net saving for 2018/19 is thus £8,600 (£10,200 – £1,600) and hence, overall, between the two years, Safiya has broken even!

BUT, instead of using the cash basis in 2018/19, Safiya could opt out and return to traditional accruals accounting. The transitional rules would ensure that her timing differences of £17,000 reversed but the additional restriction on her interest expenses would no longer apply. Hence, the additional cost of £8,600 in 2017/18 would be outweighed by a £10,200 saving in 2018/19 and Safiya would be £1,600 better off overall.

As we can see, switching between traditional accruals accounting and the cash basis may provide another mechanism to effectively accelerate taxable income to a year when the landlord has a lower marginal tax rate and defer deductible expenditure to a year when they have a higher marginal tax rate: thus producing overall savings.

However, in some cases, this will come at a cost with potential 'absolute' losses of tax relief on some expenses.

Furthermore, the whole process is rather complex to say the least!

Lightning Source UK Ltd.
Milton Keynes UK
UKOW01f1620070817
306853UK00001B/10/P

9 781911 020158